Karen McGrane

GOING RESPONSIVE

D0055216

MORE FROM A BOOK APART

Visit abookapart.com for our full list of titles.

Publisher: Jeffrey Zeldman
Designer: Jason Santa Maria
Executive Director: Katel LeDû
Editor: Nicole Fenton
Copyeditor: Caren Litherland
Proofreader: Lisa Maria Martin
Compositor: Rob Weychert
Ebook Producer: Ron Bilodeau

ISBN: 978-1-9375573-0-0

A Book Apart
New York, New York
http://abookapart.com

10 9 8 7 6 5 4 3 2 1

TABLE OF CONTENTS

FOREWORD

IT'S DIFFICULT TO get your arms around the web, because it doesn't have any edges. I mean this in a few different ways. First, the web's structure is made up of links on top of links, so it sprawls out in every direction. Second, the screens we use to access the web can scroll every which way, offering us rivers of news, status updates, emails, and—admit it—puppy photos. And, more recently, those of us who make things for the web have had to devise strategies that support an ever-increasing glut of devices, screen sizes, and contexts. Normally, this amount of variability would drive a person mad with complications—and, believe me, it did that to many of us. But this complexity was the sign of opportunity. Along came responsive design, which turned an untenable situation into a chance to re-conceive what we make for the web. I suspect you've heard all about this, and that's why you're holding this book.

Fortunately for you, there is no finer person to guide you along than Karen McGrane. She's been keeping her hands on the warm clay of the web for twenty years. The range of her expertise is important. As you dive into your responsive project, you'll notice how deeply braided together content, presentation, and development are in your decision-making process. No choices happen independently. Remember: there are no edges, so all your decisions live in several places in many forms. And there's no better way to learn how to navigate these choices than to be introduced by someone who understands all the elements at play and can speak across the disciplines. That's Karen.

Responsive projects require clear goals, frequent communication, and solid collaboration. This leads me to the last way the web encourages edgelessness—it blurs the lines between the disciplines that make the web. Yet again, a complexity offers us a new opportunity: by making things for others, we get to learn how to better work with each other. This is the true benefit of going responsive. I can't wait to see what you make.

—Frank Chimero

INTRODUCTION

MANY FINE BOOKS out there will tell you how to design and build a responsive website. This isn't one of them.

Wait! Don't throw the book away yet!

There's more to "going responsive" than fluid grids, flexible images, and media queries. Indeed, most organizations that have implemented a responsive design report that the design and development decisions were *the easy part*. The hard part is getting the organization aligned on what it means to design for all devices equally.

Going responsive requires everyone—everyone!—to approach the design and development process with a new perspective. Long-simmering conflicts about whose "thing" gets priority on the homepage must be addressed, head-on. Site speed stops being the concern of a few heroic developers and becomes something that guides decisions throughout the process. Flabby old content can't be shoved into stretchy new responsive clothes, so your editorial process and workflow must evolve.

Your entire organization must work differently to pull off a successful responsive redesign. Teams take on the challenge of designing and reviewing multiple breakpoints instead of a single fixed-width design. Design decisions must now be grounded in a style guide or pattern library, which must be created, maintained, and enforced. Stakeholders accustomed to reviewing Photoshop comps are instead expected to provide feedback on interactive prototypes. Organizations discover they must move staff into new roles, hire new people, even create new reporting relationships to manage this process effectively.

These changes may come as a surprise to executives who are accustomed to dealing with the web design and development process at arm's length. They gave their okay to go responsive—surely everything else is just an implementation detail? Unfortunately, no magic wand can take an existing website and automagically make it work across platforms and devices. Responsive design can't be implemented by hardworking designers and developers without support and buy-in from the rest of the organization. Pulling off a responsive design requires a new way of solving problems and making decisions.

This is a good thing. The promise of responsive design isn't just that organizations get a website that works across multiple devices. Responsive design forces companies to fix what's broken—in their content, design, workflow, and team structure. Pulling off a large-scale responsive redesign means learning to work more effectively and efficiently, which can set your team up for greater success in the future. You may never get a better chance to revamp how you work—let's take advantage of this opportunity.

WHAT YOU'LL GET FROM THIS BOOK

This book is based on research and interviews with dozens of companies that have successfully managed a responsive redesign. More and more companies are planning to go responsive in the next couple of years. Smart organizations will avoid the pitfalls and gain from the experience of people who have been there before. Whether you're managing the process, making decisions that affect the website, or a member of the design and development team that will bring it to life, this book will give you an overview of what you're in for.

- If you're a decision-maker—perhaps a project or product manager, stakeholder, or executive—and you're looking for information about what responsive design means for you, you've come to the right place. This book gives guidance on how to make good decisions when leading a responsive redesign. Your goal is to deliver a better website—one that works better for your business and your users.
- If you're a designer or developer looking for ways to work more effectively with the rest of your team when executing a responsive design, you've also come to the right place. If you need help explaining to your managers or stakeholders how and why this process is different, this book should come in handy—buy them a copy!

- If you're a writer or editor who wants to know how a responsive redesign can help you clean up and prioritize content, you've arrived at—dare I say it—the right place. Many organizations report that editing and managing content are the primary challenges they face with going responsive, so you're not alone.

WHAT YOU WON'T GET FROM THIS BOOK

Responsive design is a huge topic, and the explicit goal of this book is to look at how it affects people and processes outside of specific design and development techniques. Many of the issues typically considered to be at the heart of responsive design are not covered here. Fortunately, these topics have been discussed at length by other people, and you can find useful resources about them in the back of the book.

- If you're looking for help with how to actually design and build a responsive website, you'll be sadly disappointed by this book. There isn't a single line of code here. Many excellent writers—all more qualified than I am to address the specifics of how to build a responsive site—have covered this subject at length.
- If you're contrasting responsive design with other options, like a separate mobile website or native apps, you won't get a completely unbiased perspective here. The title of this book is *Going Responsive,* not *Evaluating Your Options for Mobile.* I will present research and data to help teams make a persuasive case for responsive over the alternatives.
- If you're digging deep into mobile development, web performance, or device detection, consider this the *CliffsNotes* version of some of the in-depth discussions taking place today. The purpose of this book is to help make those debates relevant to everyone, so please forgive me while I try to stay out of the weeds.

WHY YOU SHOULD LISTEN TO ME

Since the spring of 2014, Ethan Marcotte—the guy who invented the whole responsive web design thing—and I have been talking to companies of all shapes and sizes about how they implement responsive design. We've hosted workshop sessions with major corporations, including Expedia, the Associated Press, and CIBC, to help work through their most pressing concerns. Ethan and I also host a podcast series, fittingly called *A Responsive Web Design Podcast,* in which we interview people who have pulled off large-scale responsive projects at companies like Google, Starbucks, Fidelity Investments, and Condé Nast (http://bkaprt.com/gr/00-01/). I've talked with dozens of organizations about their stumbling blocks and successes along the road to responsive, and this book is a synthesis of what I've learned from them.

Beyond that, I've spent my entire career helping organizations understand and adapt to working on the web. Much of the conversation to date about responsive design has focused on specific development challenges. I'm not a web developer, and I'll admit that the nuts and bolts of implementation are not my forte. But I am an excellent translator between the people who push the web forward and the people whose jobs and businesses are affected by it. It's a privilege to walk so many organizations through this latest wave of change.

Let's start by looking at the arguments for going responsive—and the main arguments against it. Even if you're convinced that responsive design is the way to go, understanding its benefits, risks, and tradeoffs will help you make the case to your team.

MAKE THE CASE

> *" You've probably heard this before, but it really was a no-brainer to go responsive."*
> —**SARAH THOMPSON**, Seventh Generation (http://bkaprt.com/gr/01-01/)

ONE OF THE MOST common ways I hear people describe the decision to go responsive is "it was a no-brainer." For many organizations, it's less a question of whether to go responsive than a question of *when* and *how*.

Other teams are less confident in making this decision—which is understandable, since the choice to go responsive will affect people and processes throughout the organization. What about alternatives to responsive design, like a separate mobile website or native apps? Will a responsive website be able to meet the potentially differing needs of "mobile" and "desktop" users? Will responsive design be more difficult or costly to implement—and is it worth it? Convincing the interested parties that responsive design is the way to go may be a project in itself.

Whether your organization is convinced that responsive design is the right solution or you're still trying to make the case, the decision is never actually a "no-brainer." Understanding how responsive design will fit into your overall digital ecosystem will help you frame the benefits and plan for risks. And understanding that responsive design isn't an all-or-nothing prospect—but in fact plays nicely with strategies that also include native apps and even adaptive solutions—will help resolve some difficult debates and keep decision-makers focused on the goal at hand, which is building a website that works across platforms.

Even teams that have bought into responsive design as an approach say they need to spend time building a shared understanding of what responsive means and how they will work differently. Every organization should invest some time at the start of the process understanding how a responsive redesign will fit into their broader digital lifecycle and revenue model. Even if it *seems* like a no-brainer, a little strategic thinking now will pay off later.

In this chapter, we'll look at arguments for and against responsive design. Even if your mind is made up to go responsive, you'll probably come up against these debates with your team, so it's worth understanding the pros and cons.

WHY GO RESPONSIVE?

Let's assume your organization is already convinced that mobile is important. If you're still fighting that battle, turn to the comprehensive research in *Mobile is Eating the World* from Benedict Evans, partner at Andreessen Horowitz, for all the data you'll ever need to explain why mobile is mandatory (http://bkaprt. com/gr/01-02/).

The question then becomes: "Why go responsive?" Why should you build a single website that fluidly serves all devices? (You can arm yourself with talking points in both PowerPoint and PDF formats: http://bkaprt.com/gr/01-03/).

Device diversity has exploded

Who knew fixed-width design was so easy? Back when we started advocating for web standards, we had two major platforms, maybe three or four browsers to consider. We could get away with designing for one primary screen resolution. Those halcyon days are gone, and they're never coming back.

Fragmentation of device types, browsers, and screen sizes on mobile means that we've leveled up in complexity. Today, we're designing for smartphones, tablets, and desktop computers. Soon, we may be dealing with emerging form factors like watches, interactive televisions, or headsets. The sheer diversity of new devices—with their endless variety of operating systems, form factors, input mechanisms, and functionality—means that we must let go of device-specific design decisions and take a more holistic view. In *Responsive Web Design*, Ethan Marcotte wrote:

> *Responsive design is not about "designing for mobile." But it's not about "designing for the desktop" either. Rather, it's about adopting a more flexible, device-agnostic approach to designing for the web (http://bkaprt.com/gr/01-04/).*

You didn't think people were buying all these new devices and not using them, did you? Many websites today see around 50% of their traffic from smartphone and tablet devices (**FIG 1.1**). That number has increased dramatically over the past few years—and it's never going back down. (Look at your own analytics data to see how these the numbers shake out.)

Our love of mobile devices has somewhat surprisingly not come at the expense of desktop use. The amount of time we spend on desktop or laptop computers (roughly two and a half hours per day) has remained consistent, even as mobile use has skyrocketed. Time we spend with mobile devices has taken away from time we spend with print media—and probably family time, exercise, and sleep—but not desktop computers (**FIG 1.2**).

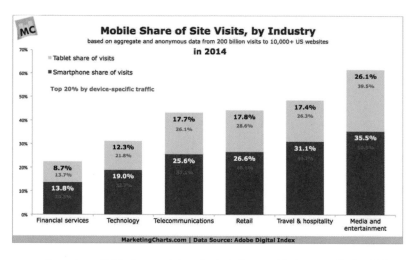

FIG 1.1: Percentage of visits from mobile varies by industry, with the top 20% of publishers seeing an astonishing 90.4% of traffic from smartphone and tablet users (http://bkaprt.com/gr/01-05/).

Device fragmentation is here to stay—we will never again live in a world where we can design for one screen size. (Well, we never lived in a world where everyone looked at the web in the same way: we just pretended we did because it made our lives easier.) It's time to give up this consensual hallucination that we can plan designs around a single screen size—or even a few different fixed-width layouts.

Tailoring to the device is harder than it seems

During our workshops, Ethan Marcotte asks: "What are the three most common words used during a responsive design project?" The answer: *mobile, tablet,* and *desktop.* Teams can easily spend hours obsessing over these form factors. But, Ethan goes on to say, these are the three *least helpful* words to use during the design process.

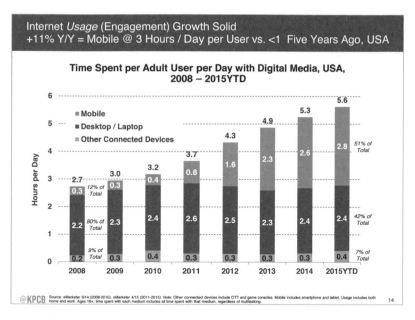

FIG 1.2: Since the dawn of the smartphone age, desktop use has remained consistent while mobile use has grown dramatically. Each now represents about half of our time spent using digital media (http://bkaprt.com/gr/01-06/).

Because we want to provide the best possible experience on the three most common form factors, it makes instinctive sense to try to tailor the experience to the device type. In this case, though, our intuition is wrong.

It's quite difficult—if not impossible—to accurately determine the type of device or browser from the client side. Sounds crazy, right? It's one of the most unintuitive aspects of defining a mobile strategy. It seems like the one thing we should be able to know with certainty is the type of device someone is holding—or at the very least its make and model—but manufacturers and browsers don't make that easy. Devices don't broadcast "I'm a tablet!" over the internet.

Even the information we *can* get is an unreliable stand-in for device type:

- **Physical screen size** does not necessarily tell us what type of device it is. It's tempting to assume that smaller screens are smartphones and larger screens are desktops or laptops, but with larger phones becoming more popular, where do you draw the line between a smartphone and a tablet? If you think you can design for a fixed-width screen size on smartphones, just remember all the times you've rotated your phone.
- **Pixel density** also varies across devices. The same physical form factor may have double the pixels—as in a Retina display—so the object in the user's hand may appear smaller than its physical screen dimensions (**FIG 1.3**). Some high-definition smartphones have higher screen resolutions than laptops. (Fun fact: iOS *icons* are now larger than the *entire screen* of the original Macintosh computer.)
- **Input modes** may seem like a way to identify different device types—smartphones and tablets use touch, while laptops and desktops use a keyboard and a mouse. But as with so many other aspects of mobile devices, input cannot be detected reliably. With more smartphones using styluses and laptop computers offering touch input—not to mention that one guy I saw at the airport with a keyboard, mouse, and external hard drive attached to his Android tablet—it's risky to think we can assume anything about device type from input modes.
- **Connection speed** doesn't really tell us anything about the device or its capabilities. (And—I'm beginning to sound like a broken record here—we have no reliable way to detect connection speed on the client side.) It's tempting to think we might send a scaled-down version of the website to slower devices, presuming that they're smartphones on cellular networks. I'm a frequent traveler, and I can confirm that hotel and airplane Wi-Fi on my laptop often rivals the slowest cellular speeds.
- **User agent detection** seems like a reasonably good way to determine device type. Developers can detect the browser

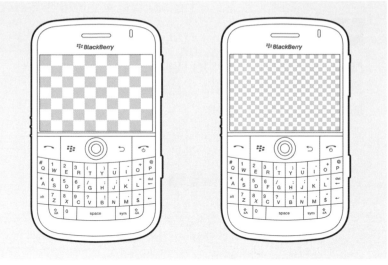

FIG 1.3: Two devices of the same physical size but different pixel densities, one with a 320×240 resolution and the other with a 640×480 resolution (http://bkaprt.com/gr/01-07/).

from the *UA string*. But user agent detection is unreliable, because there are characteristics you can't determine from the UA string. (For example, you can't tell the difference between an iPad and an iPad mini, or between iPhones with different pixel densities.) Even Google says that relying on user agent detection "is generally an error-prone technique" (http://bkaprt.com/gr/01-08/). "Browser spoofing" is a common practice—browsers sometimes lie in order to trick web servers into sending them information they might not see otherwise. Imagine your HR department mandated the company intranet only be used on Windows and Internet Explorer, even though the site would work fine in other browsers. Browsers learned to lie and say they're IE. Today, Samsung has no incentive to let you make a website that only works on iOS devices—even websites that say they're "Made for iPad." It's a tough thing to accept, but browsers are probably lying to you (**FIG 1.4**).

FIG 1.4: Microsoft's long-awaited replacement for Internet Explorer would gain nothing by naming itself in its user agent string—no sites are designed to work on it. So it names every other browser instead (http://bkaprt.com/gr/01-09/).

- **Device detection libraries** like WURFL or Netbiscuits provide the ability to identify device types and capabilities—but at a price. Relying on solutions that require you to pay for access to a proprietary library are risky—especially since there are alternatives that don't require device detection. (We'll dive into the risks of device detection a bit more in an upcoming section on managing a separate mobile website, also known as an *m-dot site*.)

Our inability to reliably and accurately know what type of device someone is holding makes designing and developing for specific device types quite difficult—if not impossible.

In fact, the only thing we can *reliably* know is the size of the browser window. That's it!

Great news: that's all we need. One of the strongest arguments for responsive design is that decisions about how to present information revolve around what we can actually know about the screen size and capabilities of the device. Based on that information, responsive design ensures that the website renders fluidly and readably in relation to the size of the browser window. Rather than basing our decision-making and design processes on fragile or inaccurate assumptions about device types, responsive design ensures that the site will work on every screen size.

Users want and need the same information on all devices

Even if determining device type is difficult, surely we should make every effort to provide the best user experience, right? In conference rooms everywhere, teams debate whether "mobile users" and "desktop users" need different content, features, or navigation—different experiences for different devices. Because a responsive approach means sending essentially the same website to everyone, regardless of device, an argument that mobile and desktop users have distinct needs is often an argument against responsive design.

Trouble is, that gut instinct that mobile users need something different isn't necessarily backed up by research or data. Companies waste a lot of time trying to imagine how what a smartphone user wants differs from what a desktop user wants. Responsive design makes that decision a snap—just serve the same website to everyone.

Turns out users don't want *you* to decide what they get on which device (**FIG 1.5**). They want what they want when they want it—a seamless experience across devices, according to this study by ExactTarget (now Salesforce Marketing Cloud) (http://bkaprt.com/gr/01-10/, PDF):

> By far, access to content "any way I want" is consumers' most important criteria when rating mobile brand experiences. In fact, 91% of consumers say access to content any way they want is important to them. 83% of consumers also say a seamless experience across all their devices is important to them— and this number increases when considering just those who own both a smartphone or a tablet (87% of consumers who rated this factor as important owned both devices).

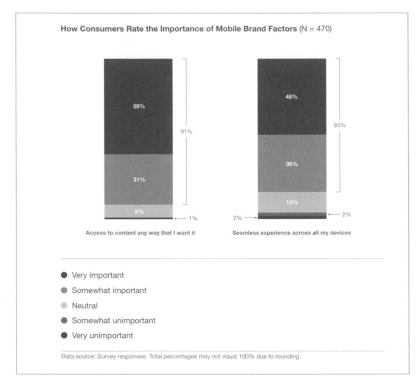

How Consumers Rate the Importance of Mobile Brand Factors (N = 470)

Access to content any way that I want it — 59%, 31%, 8%, 1%, 91%

Seamless experience across all my devices — 48%, 36%, 13%, 2%, 2%, 83%

- ● Very important
- ● Somewhat important
- ● Neutral
- ● Somewhat unimportant
- ● Very unimportant

Data source: Survey responses. Total percentages may not equal 100% due to rounding.

FIG 1.5: 91% of consumers say "access to content any way that I want it" is important to them. Our job is to provide a good experience on every device.

The device doesn't tell you anything about the user's context or intent. Have you ever used your smartphone while sitting on your couch—or at your desk, within arm's reach of your computer? Of course you have. Google reports that 77% of mobile searches take place at home or at work—not on the go (http://bkaprt.com/gr/01-11/). Why would someone want different search results or information simply because they picked up the closest device within reach?

People also need the same content and functionality on each device because they use multiple devices to complete a task. Have you ever started researching or shopping on a mobile device, then completed the task or transaction later on your desktop? Google reports that 90% of people start a task on one device, and complete it on another (http://bkaprt.com/gr/01-12/, PDF). As you might expect, people regularly do this kind of device-switching for common activities, like browsing the internet (81%) or social networking (72%). Certain categories like retail (67%), financial services (46%), and travel (43%) also seem to support this type of sequential use of different devices. Why should they get different information—or different offers or discounts—on different devices?

Cross-device behavior in people who own multiple devices is one argument for serving the same content and functionality to everyone, but what about the needs of mobile-only users? Pew Research found that 15% of smartphone-owning Americans have few options for going online other than mobile (http://bkaprt.com/gr/01-13/). Why should they be treated like second-class citizens and not be given access to the same information and services as desktop users?

Industry-wide trends are one thing, but what if your company is different? It might be—but it probably isn't. When companies across every industry look at their data, they find that people look for the same information and complete the same tasks on every size of device.

Enterprise corporations

Enterprise businesses—even those with complex service offerings—report that user needs are, in fact, not all that different between mobile and desktop. After evaluating user behavior across devices, Chris Balt, Senior Web Product Manager at Microsoft, reported:

> *Our data shows us quite plainly and clearly that the behavior of people on mobile devices is really not all that different than the behavior of people on the desktop. The things they are seeking to do and the tasks they are seeking to accomplish are really quite the same (http://bkaprt.com/gr/01-14/).*

Rather than wasting time debating how the needs of mobile and desktop users were different, Microsoft decided it would be faster and easier to deliver the same experience to everyone using responsive design.

Publishers

News organizations like Quartz have also found little difference in behavior between mobile and desktop users. Regarding the mobile-versus-desktop debate, Zach Seward, VP of Product and Executive Editor at Quartz, said, "We worried about this more in the past, that there was a big difference, and frankly I don't know that there really is one. They are the same people, just at different parts of their day" (http://bkaprt.com/gr/01-15/). While publishers have data showing that people prefer different devices at different times of day, that's not an argument for delivering different content to mobile and desktop users. Given that budgets are tight, valuable resources should be spent on editorial processes and infrastructure upgrades that provide more value than device-specific targeting.

Financial services

Financial services firms like Fidelity have moved away from the mindset that "no one will ever want to do that on their phone." Based on careful analysis of their data showing how customers use different devices to transact with Fidelity, Stephen Turbek, SVP, User Experience Design, concluded: "We've been pleasantly surprised by people's willingness to complete complex financial transactions on all the form factors, even on a phone" (http://bkaprt.com/gr/01-16/). Rather than try to pick and choose the subset of features they imagined a "mobile user" would want, they implemented responsive design to give everyone equal access to everything.

Retail

Retailers may fret about offering different experiences to shoppers at home and in stores. Monika Piotrowicz, Front-end Development Lead at Shopify, said that's not how the company thinks about user needs and goals:

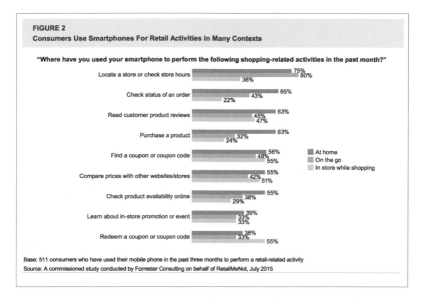

FIGURE 2
Consumers Use Smartphones For Retail Activities In Many Contexts

"Where have you used your smartphone to perform the following shopping-related activities in the past month?"

Base: 511 consumers who have used their mobile phone in the past three months to perform a retail-related activity
Source: A commissioned study conducted by Forrester Consulting on behalf of RetailMeNot, July 2015

FIG 1.6: Shoppers use their phones to research products and interact with retailers in every context.

I don't think that users on different devices have fundamentally different needs, requirements, or experiences. What's much more important to us is to look at pages and the specific goals any user may have on that type of page, rather than starting that conversation with, "Is the user on a mobile or a desktop device?" (http://bkaprt.com/gr/01-17/).

Responsive design provides a foundation that allows anyone—anywhere, on any device—to do research and complete transactions.

Research from Forrester found that for shoppers, the smartphone is now the primary device they use to interact with retailers in every context (**FIG 1.6**). Shoppers perform a variety of retail tasks at home, on the go, and in stores (http://bkaprt.com/gr/01-18/, PDF).

Intranets

Company intranets might seem like a clear-cut case for offering different content to mobile and desktop users—after all, the primary use case will be employees sitting at their company workstations. Mike Donahue, User Experience Architect at Citrix, led the design of their responsive intranet. He spent time explaining to the team that it was more important to focus on meeting user needs, regardless of platform, rather than to say "they're only going to do this if they're on desktop":

> *You just don't know what people are going to need at any given point in time. To get people to understand that, one of the use cases we shared was one of our managers. His wife had gotten sick and had to go to the hospital. Suddenly he needed some information about his insurance, and he couldn't get to it while he was not connected to the network at the office (http:// bkaprt.com/gr/01-19/).*

Travel

Even travel companies—the most "mobile" use case that exists—report that they don't necessarily see the need to tailor the experience to the device. Scott Kelton Jones, VP, Global User Experience Design at Expedia, said, "I believe that people will do anything on any device if you give them the functionality and you make it easy enough." That belief, he continued, has been confirmed by their research and testing:

> *What we've discovered as we do our ethnography research, our lab studies, as we watch the mechanics of our sites from an analytics perspective: people make the same decisions regardless of the context (http://bkaprt.com/gr/01-20/).*

Virgin America, Airbnb, and Marriott all report that responsive design makes it possible to deliver a consistent experience to users, whether they're sitting in their home office or in the front seat of a car.

Debating whether mobile and desktop users need different information is a distraction. Treating everyone equally is not only easier and more efficient, but it also delivers more value to the organization—and to the customer. Users want and need the same information on every device they own. Responsive design is the simplest way to deliver the best experience.

A single website is easier to maintain

"Sure, maintaining multiple versions of our website sounds like a great way to use our limited resources!"—said no one, ever. Most web teams I know are resource-constrained, and there's never enough time or money to do all the things they wish they could do.

Responsive design also provides a better experience for the team responsible for building and maintaining the website. Tina Alexander, formerly Director, Product Development for Time.com, explained that reducing the burden on an already overworked web staff was the main selling point when she led the responsive redesign of Celebrity Cruises:

> We think about how we optimize our resources and we usually don't have enough. This has been true of everywhere I've worked. We had to say, "What's the best way to get the biggest bang for our buck?" A framework of responsive web gave us the opportunity to respond more quickly to device changes and to make sure our content was updated across all platforms. Reducing the management costs and maintaining a more consistent presence was perhaps the most winning point we made in our discussions (http://bkaprt.com/gr/01-21/).

Responsive design concentrates your efforts, unifying development into a single codebase. Your entire team is pulling in one direction, rather than being fragmented across platforms and device types. Your investment goes further, enabling greater focus on developing new features—not to mention testing and refining existing experiences—because you're not splitting your attention and resources. When a new device comes on the market, you won't need to scramble to figure out how to deal with it—a responsive website will just work.

BBC News decided to go responsive as a way to solve a problem with product rollouts. Previously, release schedules were staggered, which meant that each platform had to wait its turn to be updated, or that team sizes needed to be doubled or tripled to meet demand:

> Companies can outsource or temporarily expand their teams to build things in parallel, which isn't free, but when the money dries up you'll have twice or thrice the amount of code to maintain and extend, which also isn't free or sustainable. You'll be chasing your tail whatever you pick unless you've got enough developers to build and maintain a few versions of everything (http://bkaprt.com/gr/01-22/).

By shifting to a responsive design, a single unified team can work together to build a single website that serves everyone equally.

One Web

This triad of arguments—dealing with device diversity, supporting user behavior across devices, and implementing unified development processes—can be summed up as a larger philosophical perspective: there is only One Web. The essence of the web is its fluidity and flexibility, and responsive design extends that core concept across different screen sizes and device types.

The W3C recommendation for Mobile Best Practices includes this principle:

> One Web means making, as far as is reasonable, the same information and services available to users irrespective of the device they are using. However, it does not mean that exactly the same information is available in exactly the same representation across all devices (http://bkaprt.com/gr/01-23/).

For many of us, the value of One Web goes beyond making development and publishing processes easier to manage. One

Web represents a fundamental philosophy that champions openness and web standards, ensuring that what we publish is accessible to everyone, regardless of location, physical ability, connection speed, or device type. This approach makes our efforts future-proof—or at least future-friendly (http://bkaprt.com/gr/01-24/). One Web means truly embracing the nature of the web as its own medium, with its own principles, rules, and values.

Your CEO's eyes may glaze over at this high-minded idealism. A Forrester report titled "Analyzing The Value Of Responsive Web Design Can Be Messy" stated, "The skeptics will simply see through the One Web message." But even those who don't embrace the One Web ideology can get behind its business value, as the report went on to say:

The One Web message is more than kicking the ROI [return on investment] can down the road. One Web is valuable for both philosophical and practical reasons. Philosophically, your digital experience efforts are constantly being pulled in different directions. The One Web message will frame the RWD [responsive web design] question in the appropriate light: If our customers are expecting a coherent experience across touchpoints, why are we siloing efforts by a narrow device category definition? Practically, One Web reinforces the needs for unified systems, processes, and teams that drive real-world cost savings and digital business efficiencies (http://bkaprt.com/gr/01-25/, PDF, requires purchase).

Google recommends responsive design

I have an alert set up to email me new articles about responsive design. I receive several each day, but they exploded in the spring of 2015, in the run-up to Google changing its algorithm to rank mobile-friendly sites more highly—hyperbolically referred to as "Mobilegeddon" (http://bkaprt.com/gr/01-26/). This change only affects searches conducted on mobile devices, but it's estimated that around half of Google's search traffic is now mobile (http://bkaprt.com/gr/01-27/). While the web design and development community has been discussing responsive design

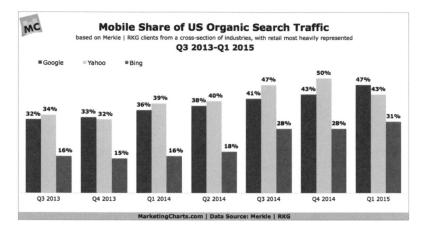

FIG 1.7: Since the end of 2013, mobile traffic to Google and Yahoo search engines has increased from roughly one-third to about half (http://bkaprt.com/gr/01-28/).

since 2010, Mobilegeddon got the attention of the mainstream (**FIG 1.7**).

Responsive design is Google's recommended approach for building mobile websites (http://bkaprt.com/gr/01-29/). It's worth noting that Google doesn't penalize sites using other methods—adaptive designs and m-dot sites with appropriate redirects still earn the label *mobile-friendly* (http://bkaprt.com/gr/01-30/). But Google recognizes that a responsive site can make link sharing easier for users and improve load time over the alternatives. Responsive also makes Google's job easier, because they only need to crawl and index a single website.

Businesses get more value from responsive design

Let's cut to the chase. For many executives, the argument that responsive design streamlines internal processes or makes for a better user experience will never be as persuasive as the argument that responsive design produces better business results (**FIG 1.8**).

A study by the Aberdeen Group showed that companies that implement responsive design achieve far better year-over-year

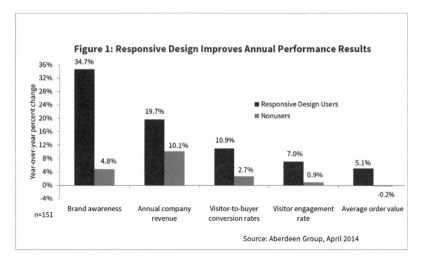

Figure 1: Responsive Design Improves Annual Performance Results

Source: Aberdeen Group, April 2014

FIG 1.8: Responsive design performed better on every metric in this analysis of 151 retail websites.

performance in key metrics like brand awareness, conversion rate, and annual company revenue (http://bkaprt.com/gr/01-31/, requires registration).

If you can't wait to see how this story turns out, skip to the end of Chapter 6 for even more data and success stories.

ALTERNATIVES TO RESPONSIVE DESIGN

Of course, responsive design is not the only option for getting on mobile. Debates about how to develop the right mobile strategy can be paralyzing. I know organizations that have struggled for years and *still* don't have a mobile website, because no one can agree on the right way to think about the problem. Other organizations have taken a scattershot approach, rolling out mobile websites and native apps—sometimes dozens of them—with no coherent approach for evaluating their success and governing them over time.

When people debate the right strategy for mobile, why do they disagree? What are they fighting about? Let's look at the three strategies that are commonly cited as alternatives to responsive design.

- **Apps:** native applications built for a specific platform.
- **M-dot sites:** separate mobile websites delivered on their own subdomain.
- **Adaptive solutions:** serving different content or code to users based on device, context, or other personalized criteria.

Apps

The ongoing fight in the Dead Horse Division is whether companies should build mobile websites or native apps. I hope I'm not giving away any spoilers when I tell you that I believe organizations should build for the web using responsive design. (You probably picked that up from the title of the book.)

"But mobile users spend most of their time using apps!" A widely cited 2014 study by Flurry showed that the average user spent two hours and forty-two minutes each day on a mobile device, but merely twenty-two minutes (or 14%) of that time in a browser (http://bkaprt.com/gr/01-32/). For many, this represents the death knell of the website, and a call for companies large and small to invest in building native apps (**FIG 1.9**).

Cut to a montage of the web working out, training hard, getting ready to fight back. What makes the web-versus-app fight more equal than those numbers suggest?

- The mobile web sees twice as much traffic than apps, and is growing 1.2 times faster, according to a report by Morgan Stanley (http://bkaprt.com/gr/01-33/, PDF). Apps offer higher engagement, but the web provides reach.
- Users spend 80% of their time in *just five* apps. Unless your name is Facebook, YouTube, Google Maps, Pandora, or Gmail, you're not likely to cash in on the app craze, according to data from Forrester cited in Mobile Marketer (http://bkaprt.com/gr/01-34/).

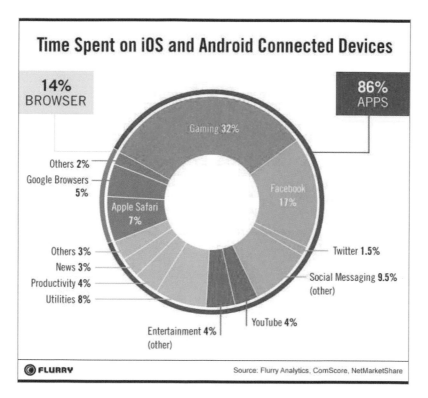

Time Spent on iOS and Android Connected Devices

14% BROWSER

86% APPS

Gaming 32%

Others 2%
Google Browsers 5%

Apple Safari 7%

Facebook 17%

Others 3%
News 3%
Productivity 4%
Utilities 8%

Twitter 1.5%

Social Messaging 9.5% (other)

Entertainment 4% (other)

YouTube 4%

FLURRY

Source: Flurry Analytics, ComScore, NetMarketShare

FIG 1.9: Only 14% of users' time is spent in a browser, compared with all the time users spend in apps. We should just shut the web down.

- Studies of mobile app usage overlook web usage inside an app browser. How much time spent on Twitter is really spent on the web? In-app browser usage is an argument *for* responsive design, not for investing in a standalone app.
- Users don't believe they use apps more often than the web. A study from the Interactive Advertising Bureau (IAB) found that only 18% of users self-report spending most of their time in apps—a big discrepancy between perceived and actual usage (http://bkaprt.com/gr/01-35/, PDF).

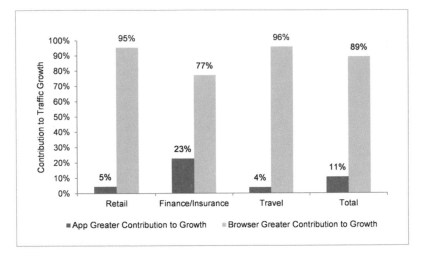

FIG 1.10: Whether it's from search, social, or email, visitors land on your website—which means it's the widest part of your customer acquisition funnel and the biggest driver of growth (http://bkaprt.com/gr/01-33/, PDF).

- News flash: users have always spent most of their time on desktop computers using apps. And yet, no one ever found that cause for alarm—or an indication that the web is dead.

Let's not give up on the web just yet.

That's not to say native apps aren't also an important part of many mobile strategies. The reason this fight is so tired is that successful companies see web and app as complementary, not competitive (**FIG 1.10**). Airbnb, the *Guardian,* and OpenTable all complement their responsive websites with native apps for their most engaged users. (Of course, successfully maintaining a website and native apps requires companies to have the budget and resources to devote to multiple teams, codebases, and release schedules—not everyone does.)

Whether or not you choose to invest in a native app, you still need a website. Benedict Evans from Andreessen Horowitz weighed in on the web-versus-app debate to say that although apps are optional, the web is not:

You should have a website that works well on mobile regardless of whether you also have an app, and that site should give your complete proposition, since that of course is where links from Google and Facebook will take people. In either of these cases— whether you have an app and a website or just a website, you should presume that your customers will engage with you only on mobile (http://bkaprt.com/gr/01-36/).

Stop positioning these strategies as if they're in competition. For virtually every company, responsive web is the baseline— you must have a website and it must be responsive. Apps are appropriate for some companies, particularly if they have an active, engaged user base that is willing to authenticate for personalized information. It's never either/or.

M-dot sites

Another common strategy for getting on mobile has been to develop a separate mobile website and serve it on a subdomain—often m.domain.com (hence the moniker *m-dot site*). Companies then manage two different websites: typically one fixed-width website for desktop users, and a narrower site for mobile users. (Some companies add a third experience for tablet users, known as a *t-dot*. Presumably w-dot sites for watches and tv-dot sites for interactive televisions would follow.)

What's the benefit of an m-dot site? For many companies, an m-dot is a stop-gap measure to get *something* up on the mobile web while they plan for the long term. Even though an m-dot doesn't provide the best experience and usually offers less content and functionality than the desktop website, it's better than nothing.

Some organizations use the m-dot site as a testing ground for their responsive work, rolling out the responsive design in stages to smartphone and tablet users, before it eventually overtakes the desktop site and gets served to everyone. (For more information on rollout strategies, see Chapter 2.)

And yet, other people argue that a separate mobile website is the best long-term strategy. Rather than delivering a single website using responsive design, they argue that it's preferable to treat mobile and desktop as different use cases, served by different codebases and content. Since we've already covered data showing that people don't really need or want different information or functionality on mobile than they do on the desktop, let's look at some of the specific implementation tradeoffs between m-dot and responsive sites.

Performance

Site speed is the number one reason developers argue an m-dot site is preferable for mobile. Fans of the m-dot claim it is inherently faster. In a responsive site, a single codebase serves all users. With an m-dot site, developers maintain separate codebases: each device type gets sent its own HTML, CSS, and JavaScript, which means that page weights on mobile sites can be smaller than on their desktop counterparts.

But page weight is only one consideration when comparing performance between responsive and m-dot sites. Because m-dot sites usually require an initial redirect (sending users who navigate to domain.com over to m.domain.com), users perceive a delay while they wait to be redirected. (We'll talk about how to use adaptive solutions to serve different code and content to the same URL later in this chapter.)

So, m-dot or responsive design: which is faster? When Doug Sillars, Principal Architect – Mobile Application Optimization at AT&T, analyzed data from the top one thousand mobile websites, he concluded: "We should probably call it a dead heat" (http://bkaprt.com/gr/01-37/). As a general rule, m-dot sites are smaller in both page weight and number of server requests, but responsive sites are just about as fast—sometimes even faster—than m-dots.

It's a myth that the only way to make a fast-loading site on mobile is an m-dot. Good coding and decision-making practices can serve up responsive sites that are every bit as fast as any other method. (For more information on making performance a priority, see Chapter 3.)

Experience parity

I'd wager that many of the performance gains shown by m-dot sites come from delivering "less-than" experiences—sites lacking some of the features and content users expect to find on the website. Sure, developers may debate whether the HTML, CSS, and JavaScript for responsive sites can ever be as small as that of a fixed-width site. But people who cite the performance gains inherent to m-dot websites need to take into account that those sites may offer a subset of the content and features from the desktop site. It's not an apples-to-apples comparison.

Users reject websites that don't offer adequate content and functionality. In a study conducted by ExactTarget (now Salesforce Marketing Cloud) on consumer behavior on mobile, 54% of respondents said that mobile-optimized websites don't offer enough content (http://bkaprt.com/gr/01-38/, PDF).

Capital One discovered that a shocking 96% of their users were abandoning their m-dot site because it offered a paltry subset of the information available on the desktop site. After they went responsive, their mobile bounce rate decreased by 15% in the first twenty-four hours. Over time, they saw an 8% increase in conversion rate on mobile and a 17% increase on tablet—huge numbers in the credit card industry, where a single percentage point may equate to millions of dollars (http://bkaprt.com/gr/01-39/).

Server-side device detection

We've already noted that it's difficult—if not impossible—to accurately determine the type of device or the browser someone is using from the client side. To get around this, third-party companies like ScientiaMobile and NetBiscuits maintain proprietary databases of device characteristics. M-dot sites rely on server-side device detection to determine which version of the website to send to which devices. Companies that sell these products have a vested interest in convincing teams that an m-dot strategy is the right way to go.

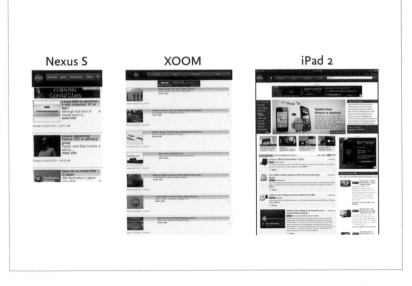

FIG 1.11: Trying to guess which layout to send to which device can result in some devices receiving an inappropriate—no, terrible—layout (http://bkaprt.com/gr/01-41/).

But the problem with device detection goes beyond the risks inherent in relying on proprietary, server-side libraries. The likelihood that we will send an inappropriate layout to a device is just too high—and the likelihood that new devices will come on the market that we haven't designed for is, well, 100% (**FIG 1.11**).

A 2014 study by Radware found that larger Android devices were more likely than iOS devices to be served an m-dot layout optimized for mobile phones. Among the top 100 retailers evaluated, 30% served the m-dot version to the Nexus 7 and 26% served it to the Galaxy Note—even though those form factors are similar to the iPad mini, to which only 6% of retailers served the m-dot version. What's worse, 20% of these m-dot sites didn't even give users the option to see the full site (http://bkaprt.com/gr/01-40/, requires registration).

As much as some people might wish to believe we can use device detection to accurately tailor designs to device type, this

FIG 1.12: You don't get to decide which device someone uses to open your m-dot URL. A user looking for cars on m.vw.com from a desktop browser gets an unexpectedly bad experience.

is an arms race we simply cannot win. Rather than depending on server-side mechanisms to solve problems with screen layout, those problems are best solved on the client side with responsive design. Even better—a completely fluid solution on the client side means that whenever new devices and screen sizes come out, the website will work without requiring a redesign.

Link sharing

Another downside of maintaining multiple domains is that it makes link sharing more difficult for users. Have you ever opened an m-dot link on your desktop computer, and wondered why the layout is borked? The layout may be optimized for mobile devices, but it's suboptimal for users who want to share links with other people, or even with themselves (**FIG 1.12**). Because separate domains make it harder to share URLs, Google "strongly recommend[s] that you serve all your sites from a single domain" (http://bkaprt.com/gr/01-42/, PDF).

Now, all of these problems are surmountable. Defining canonical URLs, setting up redirects—these techniques can help smooth out the user experience, if you have the time and resources to manage and maintain them (http://bkaprt.com/gr/01-43/). The care and feeding of your m-dot site will add up.

Organizational politics

If having a separate mobile website is so problematic, then why does this debate rage on? The answer to that question lies more in organizational structure than user experience. Companies default to having separate mobile and desktop teams to minimize conflict, giving each group their own patch of turf to play on. Ryan Shafer, formerly VP of Design and User Experience at MTV, reported that their m-dot sites were managed separately before they went responsive:

> Mobile was a separate silo in the organization. We had separate leadership and production teams managing our m-dot sites. We even had a different logo for MTV on mobile (http://bkaprt. com/gr/01-44/).

Giving separate teams their own patch of turf means that—at least in the short term—decisions can be made quickly. But the same organizations soon realize that managing and maintaining separate mobile and desktop versions of the website requires too much work for too few benefits.

The best evidence for a single responsive website is the sheer number of companies that started with a separate mobile website, threw it away, and went responsive. Capital One, the *Guardian,* the BBC, and Marriott all saw their maintenance costs go down—and customer-facing metrics improve—when they moved away from a separate mobile site. Dave Augustine, Engineering Manager at Airbnb, said:

> Take it from experience: we had a separate mobile website with a different tech stack and it turned out to be a lot of work to maintain. It fell really out of date—totally diverged from the desktop—and you don't want that. Mobile is so important to your business that you can't afford to be sending people to a poor experience. My advice is to avoid building a separate web

application just for mobile sites. Just go responsive (http:// bkaprt.com/gr/01-45/).

NPR—a company I cite in my book, *Content Strategy for Mobile,* as an organization that has gone all-in on multiplatform publishing—has pulled back from device-specific strategies on the web and instead has gone responsive. Patrick Cooper, NPR's Director of Web and Engagement, reported:

> *We had a phone website, and a tablet website, and a desktop website, and we really only maintained the desktop website because we didn't have enough resources to cover all those fronts. It just wasn't a tenable situation (http://bkaprt.com/ gr/01-46/).*

Think it's time to close the book on topics like device detection and maintaining device-specific versions of content or features? Finishing this section is like winning a pie-eating contest where the prize is more pie. "M-dot versus responsive" is the 101 version of this topic. Now, it's time to move on to the advanced version: adaptive solutions.

Adaptive solutions

Here's a riddle for you: how is adaptive like an m-dot?

At its core, responsive design upholds the ethos of One Web. Its goal is to manage one set of content and one set of code, and to deliver essentially the same experience to everyone. Adaptive is, well, not responsive. Its ethos is to deliver something *different* to the user—different content, different design—targeted to the device or based on some other criteria. For companies that want to deliver a different experience to users on desktop and mobile without signing up to maintain a separate m-dot site, adaptive is the answer.

While responsive design has a clear and consistent definition—fluid grids, flexible images, and media queries—*adaptive* means many different things depending on whom you're talking to. No clear-cut, industry-standard language defines adaptive solutions. So when someone says, "We'll solve this problem using adaptive," that's your cue to clarify what they *really* mean. (Warning: too often, people use "adaptive" as a synonym for "magic.")

Let's look at three common definitions for what people mean when they say adaptive: adaptive grids, adaptive designs, and adaptive content.

Adaptive grids

One of the most frequently used definitions of adaptive is a single codebase with a series of fixed, static layouts at different resolutions. Responsive designs are based on a fluid grid. An adaptive grid "snaps" into place at device-specific sizes (http:// bkaprt.com/gr/01-47/).

The advantage to building with adaptive grids is that teams can focus their design process on creating layouts aimed at specific device types (**FIG 1.13**). It should be clear why that's also the disadvantage of adaptive grids. Because screen sizes vary so widely, most devices will not perfectly match one of the anticipated sizes. The whole point of going responsive is that the design will fluidly cover all screen sizes.

Aiming an adaptive grid at one specific screen size or device type means that other devices are likely to receive a suboptimal layout. When new devices come on the market, teams may need to rework the design. For example, when the iPhone 6 launched with an entirely new screen size, some adaptive layouts were not optimized for it—but responsive designs fluidly adjusted to the new size.

Adaptive grids may be thought of as a way of creating somewhat device-specific layouts entirely on the client side. The next two definitions of adaptive—*adaptive designs* and *adaptive content*—get the backend involved to serve different content or functionality to the same URL.

I find it useful to say that responsive design solutions are client-side, while adaptive solutions require server-side negotiation (http://bkaprt.com/gr/01-49/). Google sometimes refers to adaptive solutions as "dynamic serving" (http://bkaprt.com/gr/01-30/). Luke Wroblewski coined the term RESS, which stands for Responsive Design and Server Side Components—this may

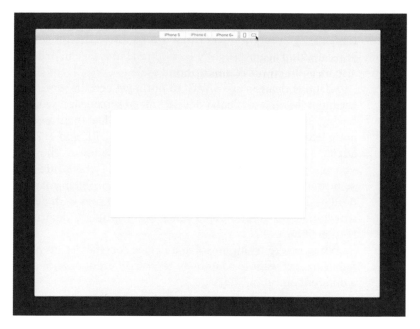

FIG 1.13: A hypothetical design application supports adaptive layouts for specific iOS device screen sizes (http://bkaprt.com/gr/01-48/).

be considered another name for adaptive (http://bkaprt.com/gr/01-50/). Client side = responsive, server side = adaptive is a general guideline, not a hard-and-fast rule. (Remember, adaptive grids are entirely client-side). But the client-side/server-side distinction moves this discussion forward by clarifying that to deliver different content or functionality, we often need to get the server involved.

Adaptive designs

In a responsive design, essentially the same front-end code is sent to every device. While a single codebase is more consistent and easier to maintain, it sometimes requires making tradeoffs in layout or presentation. If you were designing desktop-only, you might make different layout or design decisions than if you were designing responsively. Faced with some of these tradeoffs, you might decide that a responsive design should serve desktop users a slightly less optimal interface in order to also meet the needs of smartphone users.

Adaptive designs are a way to optimize certain aspects of the interface for a particular device type or screen size, without having to support a separate m-dot site. Rather than create a completely different website with its own URL and HTML, adaptive designs offer a more fine-grained solution, allowing you to serve different HTML to the same URL, which sidesteps some of the problems with m-dot sites. (One problem adaptive designs do not avoid is the aforementioned issues with device detection—this solution also relies on proprietary device-detection libraries.)

When you're trying to solve a device-specific design problem, you may want to adaptively serve a different page or even a different object on the page:

- **Serve a different page:** Specific pages or templates—like the homepage, a mobile landing page for an ad campaign, or a complex form—may be good candidates for adaptive design solutions. While the majority of pages on the website can likely be responsive, it may be more efficient to deal with a few problematic pages adaptively. Even Chris Coyier, founder and author of CSS Tricks, said he opted for a hybrid solution when developing CodePen (http://bkaprt. com/gr/01-51/). If there's anyone out there who can ninja his way through a responsive design solution, it's Chris Coyier—but he determined they were better off maintaining two different versions of certain templates to provide a better user experience on smaller and larger screen sizes.
- **Serve a different object:** A layout problem often doesn't encompass the entire page. Rather, it's only a discrete object—say, a table or media player—that wants to be different on smaller and larger devices. It's possible to use adaptive designs only for specific features, sending variations to different device types. Fidelity has used this approach to give smartphone users a readable summary of a complex table, while tablet and desktop users get the full-sized table.

Beatport serves different versions of their music player, even though the rest of the application is fully responsive (http://bkaprt.com/gr/01-52/).

If you're trying to solve a problem relating to screen size, you're better off solving it fluidly on the client side with responsive design. While adaptive designs may seem faster and easier to implement in the short term—and offer some device-specific improvements to the user experience—it's not worth the effort. Why maintain multiple design variations and get the server involved to support expensive and risky device detection to solve a problem that you can solve using responsive design alone?

When do you need to get the server involved? When you want to serve different content.

Adaptive content

In a responsive design, the exact same content gets sent to everyone on every device. When people talk about the limitations of responsive design, this is one of the most frequently cited issues. Companies often want to deliver different content, based on characteristics they can discern about the user or the device. Adaptive content is often used to serve different information to specific device types, but it can also be used to personalize content by user context or other business logic.

Adaptive content gets the CMS (or other publishing systems) involved to serve content *variations*. For more than a decade, adaptive content solutions have been used to support publishing to different platforms—imagine publishing different help text for Mac and Windows printers to web and print manuals. Today, adaptive content makes it possible to deliver different content or marketing messages according to what you know about the user—where they are, what time of day it is, or what type of device they have.

If you want to deliver different content based on some defined criteria, your content first must be *structured*. Rather than having content styled for (and locked up in) a big blob of a field—like a wiki page or PDF—adaptive content is stored as smaller, presentation-independent chunks. Storing content with finer granularity provides a number of benefits: it makes the content more flexible for reuse, as well as easier to manage and maintain. (A complete guide to creating adaptive content falls outside the scope of this book, but the process is covered at length in my book, *Content Strategy for Mobile*.)

For many companies, the main reason for seeking adaptive content is its ability to be *targeted*. With structured content, companies can create variations that can be dynamically served based on characteristics you can discern about the user or the device. Content can be targeted against three major variables:

- **Device type.** Adaptive content enables sending specific chunks of content to smartphones, tablets, and desktop— as well as televisions, digital signs, even watches and wear- ables. You can serve a shorter form of a headline or teaser to smartphones and watches, and a longer form to device types with larger screens. Adaptive content also supports mobile-specific campaign landing pages or device-specific SEO keywords, if that's what you're into. (Keep in mind that all the same problems with device detection still apply here.)
- **Context.** Devices can't tell you what the user is doing, but they can give you information from sensors that can be used to guide assumptions about user context. Based on time of day, publishers might serve different content to target users presumed to be at home or work. Location information can be used to present nearby restaurants or serve targeted offers to users in retail stores. Other device sensors could provide information about velocity, temperature, humidity, and more, and that data could be used to deliver contextual messages. But these data points are always an inadequate proxy for actual user context. For example, a device might use velocity sensors to make the assumption that a user going faster than 10 mph is in a car, but that user could be bicycling or running.
- **Personalization.** While targeting by context means looking at environmental cues from device location or other sen- sors, true personalization requires access to data about an

individual's demographics and past behavior. Whether you are excited or terrified by a future in which websites are tailored to your gender, age, race, or income, adaptive content is what will support that goal. A less dystopian vision—one that exists today—would support serving different marketing messages to customers depending on whether or not they have purchased before.

Responsive and adaptive work together

Adaptive solutions are often presented as the opposite of responsive design—I've read dozens of articles claiming that adaptive is what enables marketers to go "beyond responsive." But adaptive and responsive are not in competition—they're complementary. Adaptive content can and should be served into responsive templates. Even adaptive and responsive designs can be used together—if organizations find that a specific table or template is problematic when served responsively, then just those discrete pieces can be served adaptively.

The fact that certain scenarios may require adaptive solutions does not mean that responsive design is inadequate, or a failure. To solve the complex problems inherent in supporting all these new platforms and device types, we need every tool in our arsenal.

That said, organizations that are considering adaptive solutions should still start with responsive. Responsive design provides a foundation that works across all devices and solves the vast majority of problems. Bill W. Scott, Vice President, Next Gen Commerce at PayPal, explained that responsive is the baseline that companies must implement before moving on to adaptive solutions:

> From a design perspective as well as an engineering perspective, responsive is just table stakes. It's a default thing that should always happen. You may later decide to create a custom experience to optimize around specific mobile scenarios. But you don't have to go there first. You can start with responsive (http://bkaprt.com/gr/01-52/).

Adaptive solutions can be layered on later as needed, to solve thorny problems where one site does not fit all. Livia Labate, formerly Senior Director, User Experience Design at Marriott, reported that a responsive design served the needs of all customers, freeing the team up to focus on specialized, device-specific scenarios in the future:

> It's important to acknowledge that most activities are universal, even if there may also be device-specific needs. By having the web experience unified through a responsive approach, we cover the base scenarios across the board, and can later do a better job at handling device specifics (http://bkaprt.com/ gr/01-53/).

Responsive design offers a fluid, flexible, and future-friendly approach to dealing with the explosion of devices on the market today—and the emerging form factors and screen sizes of tomorrow. Responsive serves the needs of your customers, who benefit most from being able to get access to the same information and features on every device. It also serves the needs of your team and your business, which will see a greater return on investment from a website that's more efficient to manage and maintain. And even if you anticipate wanting to deliver adaptive solutions in the future, a responsive design provides a solid foundation.

That's the argument for responsive design in a nutshell. Now that we've made the case, let's look at how to plan a responsive project.

2 PLAN YOUR APPROACH

Stripping everything down to enable a simple and effective smartphone or tablet experience involves a level of strategic planning which many companies have not yet been able to master."
—ECONSULTANCY (IN ASSOCIATION WITH ADOBE), "Finding the Path to Mobile Maturity" (http://bkaprt.com/gr/02-01/, PDF)

WHAT'S DIFFERENT ABOUT planning a responsive project? In one sense: nothing. Responsive design is just web design, and the principles and processes we've developed over the past two decades still apply.

In another sense, responsive projects are completely different—but not because they use fluid grids and media queries. Responsive projects aren't just about building a website. They're about training your team. Implementing a new process. Educating the organization on new ways to solve problems. These activities all have value that go beyond making your website work on more devices.

When you're planning a responsive project, take the efforts required from your entire organization into account. How will you roll out the redesign? What do stakeholders and decision-makers need to do to ensure it goes smoothly? How will you structure your team—now and in the future—so that team members can collaborate effectively?

Any business leader who talks about ROI should understand: it's not just about the cost of the initiative, it's about the value returned. Companies that have delivered a successful responsive redesign say they got much more from the initiative than a website that works on smartphones—they got an organization that thinks and works differently. The real value from responsive design comes from the organizational change that happens behind the scenes.

SCOPING

Responsive design *must* take longer and cost more, right (**FIG 2.1**)? Ethan Marcotte recounted that after his book *Responsive Web Design* was published, naysayers insisted that building websites this way would triple the cost—after all, you're building a smartphone, tablet, and desktop view (http://bkaprt.com/gr/02-02/).

Organizations that have been through the process report more modest increases in scope. Project leads estimate it takes roughly 25 to 50% more time and budget to implement a responsive redesign. These figures were echoed in a Forrester report:

> Forrester has heard from AD&D [application development and delivery] leaders and their agency partners that responsive web design (RWD) takes between 20% to 50% longer (some outliers ranged up to 250% longer) than traditional desktop web design efforts (http://bkaprt.com/gr/01-25/, PDF, requires purchase).

Planning your project

When planning a responsive project, the fundamentals of web design remain the same. The activities and deliverables you typically create for a web project also apply to a responsive project. Once you adapt to some of the process changes required for

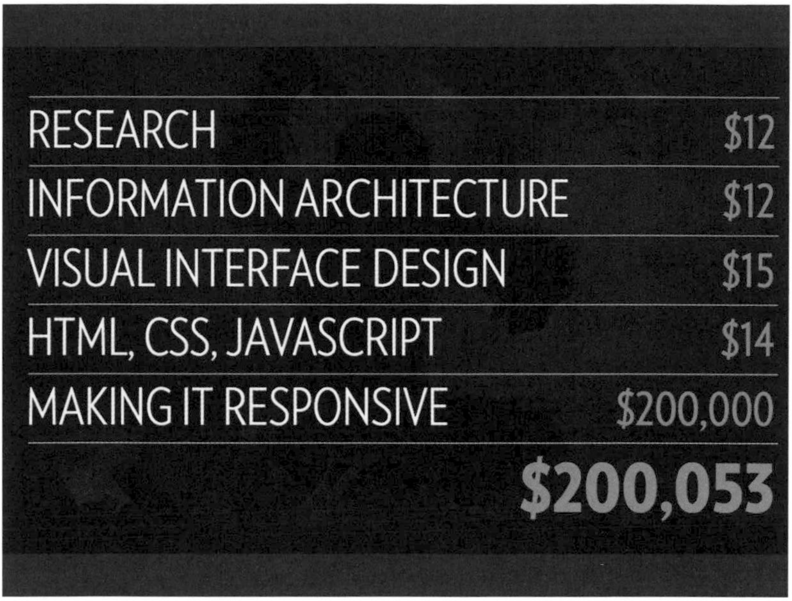

RESEARCH	$12
INFORMATION ARCHITECTURE	$12
VISUAL INTERFACE DESIGN	$15
HTML, CSS, JAVASCRIPT	$14
MAKING IT RESPONSIVE	$200,000
	$200,053

FIG 2.1: Mike Monteiro offered some helpful guidance for scoping responsive projects in his talk, "What Clients Don't Know (and Why It's Your Fault)." He's probably exaggerating. Probably (http://bkaprt.com/gr/02-03/).

going responsive, project scope will be consistent with previous efforts. Elliott Jay Stocks, Creative Director of Adobe Typekit, emphasized that responsive projects will not cost more in the long run:

> *Once you overcome that initial struggle of adapting to a new process, designing and building responsive sites needn't take any longer, or cost any more money. The real obstacle is designers and developers being set in their ways (http://bkaprt.com/gr/02-04/).*

So what are the process changes that result in that initial 25 to 50% increase in scope? The greatest effort (and most unknown risks) arise from the following:

- Training designers, developers, and other team members in new technical skills, like progressive enhancement and designing for performance. (See Chapter 3.)
- Cleaning up and paring down existing desktop content, including reformatting PDFs or Flash videos that won't work on mobile devices. (See Chapter 4.)
- Educating the entire organization about how decision-making processes change when creating a fluid design that serves all devices, rather than aiming for specific fixed-width layouts. (See Chapter 5.)
- Shifting to a way of working that focuses on building prototypes rather than static deliverables, and coaching the entire organization on being more collaborative and iterative. (See Chapter 5.)
- Testing the website across browsers, device types, and orientations. (See Chapter 6.)

Project managers may tremble at the prospect of an iterative, fluid design process with few set-in-stone checkpoints and few, if any, static deliverables. Brandon Rosage, Creative Director at Ushahidi, said that working this way actually helped them scope the project accurately and reduced the time required for review:

> *A big part of scoping our work and offering accurate estimates has been to set down some rules from the beginning—or at least expectations. One of the big changes that has helped is getting out of graphic design applications and into prototypes very, very early. That way there's less time spent asking people over email, or over Skype, to look at a picture of a design and imagine how it will work. They understand the design by seeing it in action (http://bkaprt.com/gr/02-05/).*

Budgeting beyond responsive

When evaluating the cost of a responsive redesign, keep in mind that these projects cost more because your organization is *doing* more. Along with designing and building a responsive website, many companies are tackling a wider set of problems that get bundled into a redesign. Livia Labate of Marriott remarked, "The responsive program was also a fantastic excuse to fix stuff. That was actually one of the greatest benefits of all" (http://bkaprt.com/gr/01-53/).

While the following initiatives are often included as part of a responsive redesign, it's not quite correct to blame responsive design for the additional cost and time associated with them:

- Creating and enforcing a design system or pattern library. Having these reusable patterns in place will make it easier and faster to build pages, which will reduce costs in the long run. (See Chapter 5 for more information.)
- Replacing existing backend systems, like content management systems or ecommerce systems.
- Implementing new APIs, digital asset management (DAM) systems, or other middleware to support mobile devices.

Even though responsive projects may seem to require more effort, in the years to come, we won't be comparing the cost of building something responsively against our old fixed-width approaches. Like any new methodology, there will be an initial cost associated with getting everyone up to speed—but over the long term, it won't cost more or take more time. It will just be the way teams work.

ROLLING OUT RESPONSIVE

I wish I could tell you there was one true path to rolling out a responsive redesign successfully. But from talking to dozens of organizations, it's clear that the process by which large organizations go responsive varies widely. Many different approaches will work—but you need to understand the benefits and risks of each approach.

Can you redesign the entire site at once or do you need to stage the rollout over time? Are you going to retrofit the existing desktop site or start from scratch? Will you release a beta version of the site or do a "big reveal"? To find the right option for your organization, ask yourself these questions:

- **How worried are you about existing customers on the desktop site?** Now, no one is going to answer, "Not worried even one tiny little bit." But some organizations (say, publishers) redesign relatively frequently without launching a beta version—they just flip the switch. Other organizations (say, banks) know they can't risk frustrating existing customers by introducing drastic changes without an adjustment period.
- **Are you redesigning a web application?** Don't let anyone tell you that web apps can't be made responsive. They can—but it takes time and effort. If you have large tabular presentations of data, complex form-based transaction flows, or tricky integrations with legacy backend systems, be sure to build additional time into your process.
- **Do you plan to make changes to your content?** A responsive redesign is a fantastic opportunity to clean up and pare down your existing content—you may never get a better chance to fix bloated content that isn't doing its job. That said, many organizations find they can't do everything at once, so they roll out the content cleanup in stages.
- **Do you plan to implement a new CMS or APIs?** Many organizations report that the work they've done over the past few years to replatform their publishing systems makes going responsive much simpler. But you'll need to decide whether to do the CMS or the redesign first. It's riskier and more time-consuming to do them at the same time.
- **Are your stakeholders prepared for the review process?** Some organizations use a responsive redesign to engage the entire organization in learning a new process. Others take a "better to ask forgiveness than permission" approach, rolling out the redesign first and fixing the inevitable broken pieces later.

Once you know the answers to these questions, consider your options for going responsive.

Retrofit

Doing a responsive retrofit means recoding the front end of the website with little or no change to the existing content and design.

I must confess: before I started talking to companies that launched a successful responsive retrofit, I was convinced this was the worst of all possible options, doomed to deliver a subpar experience to everyone involved. My philosophical beliefs about the "right way" to manage web processes don't always survive their encounters with the real world: I concede that a retrofit works well in some scenarios.

In general, retrofits work best when at least one of the following statements is true:

1. The content isn't going to change (much).
2. Complex web applications don't need to be redesigned.
3. A componentized framework is already in place.

Companies like Capital One, Marriott, and Nationwide Insurance have implemented responsive retrofits successfully. Doing a retrofit forced them to focus on the responsive aspects of the project without getting sidetracked by larger questions of redesigning the site, editing the content, or replatforming the CMS. For many websites, a retrofit also helps mitigate political concerns around changing or damaging the desktop experience, since it doesn't change much.

Here's how you roll out a retrofit right:

- **"Don't touch the desktop"** is a mandate often handed down to the responsive team, but this guideline is too limiting. It forces the team to work toward unnecessary design parity at the expense of making better design decisions for smaller screens.
- **"Do no harm to the desktop"** is a more realistic and achievable ambition. This gives teams the flexibility they need to make adjustments to layout, design, navigation, or content.
- **Set realistic expectations** with your team and develop a plan for making changes over the long term. Stakeholders may be surprised when they see how existing content and functionality shifts around on different screens.
- **Consider picking one section** for a complete responsive overhaul. A fully edited and redesigned section can provide a useful point of comparison with the retrofit. Picking a

section for a complete redesign will give teams experience with the process, show stakeholders what's possible, provide insight into the level of effort that can inform future scoping processes, and offer real-world data about how a fully redesigned experience will perform compared to the retrofit.

Beta release

In recent years, popular web applications like Gmail, Flickr, and Delicious launched in beta—and stayed in beta (http://bkaprt.com/gr/02-06/). This "perpetual beta" approach was a precursor to the continuous deployment practices used by many applications today to support ongoing development and testing.

Today, when teams say they're launching in beta they often mean that users can opt out of the new site at any time and return to the "classic" version of the website. This "parallel beta" approach requires significantly more time and effort to develop and review, but in return delivers the ability to roll out the redesign slowly, gathering user feedback and analytics data along the way.

Companies like Fidelity, Beatport, and the *Guardian* have invested in parallel beta releases, which gave them a way to test and learn from the responsive design over time. Stephen Turbek of Fidelity said their decision to launch in beta was crucial to their success:

> One of our first steps was to build a beta site that people could opt-in to, try out for a while, and return to the current site. The beta site was significant additional work, but iterating live on a site with millions of passionate customers would not have been the right approach. This enabled us to make changes faster and get lots and lots of user feedback (http://bkaprt.com/gr/01-16/).

Here's what needs to happen to launch a successful beta:

- **A test-and-learn culture** should already be established in your organization. Teams must be comfortable working in tight cycles of iteration and testing—most teams will need to run tests every six weeks, and even as frequently as every week or two. If you don't already work this way, building a culture of learning from research will take time and add complexity.

- **Technical architecture** and publishing infrastructure must be in place so users that can opt in and out, which can be costly.
- **Executive buy-in** from stakeholders who see the value of the beta process and are willing to invest in maintaining two versions of the site—not to mention driving traffic to two different URLs—is crucial.
- **Quality assurance testing** (QA) becomes exponentially more complex when testing on more form factors. Don't underestimate the time or staff you'll need to QA two versions of the site.
- **Rolling out the beta in stages** will help control who can access it. Alex Breuer, Creative Director at the *Guardian*, said they found that showing the beta site to users coming in through search or social "was a gentle way of introducing the new Guardian experience" (http://bkaprt.com/gr/02-07/).
- **Assume early feedback will be negative** if your beta site excludes content or functionality from the old site. Help stakeholders understand that negative feedback is not a sign of failure—in fact, getting these comments early is the whole point of the beta.

Mobile-only responsive

Another rollout strategy—often but not always implemented in the context of a beta release—is to develop a responsive website that covers all sizes of smartphones and tablets, preserving the current fixed-width site for desktop users only. In a sense, this approach is a "responsive m-dot site," but that word puzzle twists my brain into a knot, so let's not call it that. We'll call it a *mobile-only responsive site*.

A mobile-only responsive site buys an organization time to focus on larger, more complex issues. Companies know they need a site that serves mobile users, but they're afraid to hurt existing desktop traffic. But they also know the site needs a complete redesign or major backend infrastructure improvements, so they don't want to do a retrofit. In that sense, a mobile-only responsive design offers the best of both worlds. Teams can focus on getting the responsive design right, without dealing with the stakeholder politics and operational risks inherent in changing the desktop mothership.

But this approach is also the worst of both worlds—it allows stakeholders to keep believing that the desktop website is the "real" website, downplaying the large and growing population of mobile users. It also means, as with all m-dot sites, that smartphone and desktop users will suffer from the same performance hit due to server redirects.

Here's what can you do to launch a successful mobile-only responsive site:

- **Treat it like a beta** even if you're not rolling it out in stages. Have a plan for gathering data, testing, and revising the responsive site. Over time, plan for a staged rollout to desktop users.
- **Make tough choices** about content and functionality. This rollout strategy is most successful when it is used to clean up and pare down a site that's gotten out of control. If you're not prepared to make the hard decisions, just do a retrofit.
- **Educate your team** on what makes a responsive website successful. The risk with a skunkworks approach is that the "mobile" team will go off and do its own thing and the rest of the organization won't learn from the experience.
- **Make it the *real* website.** Set expectations that this process isn't about building a "mobile" website—it's about building a site that will eventually replace the desktop.
- **Know when to stop investing in the desktop site** and shift resources to the responsive site. BBC News said that continuing to work on their desktop site "sucked resources and morale and that cost us dearly by delaying our strategic move to 'Responsive News'" (http://bkaprt.com/gr/02-08/).

Section by section

Other organizations choose to start with a specific section— even one particular page or template type. Rather than doing the entire site at once, they choose to sandbox their efforts and give teams time to practice.

Which section should you start with? The answer to that question varies as widely as any other rollout approach. Some organizations report that they picked a section they knew they wanted to redesign. Celebrity Cruises started with their Destinations section, making it responsive as part of a larger effort to rewrite content and replatform the CMS (http://bkaprt.com/gr/01-21/). Other companies start with a less-popular section, a section run by stakeholders who are excited about the process, or one that gets a disproportionate amount of mobile traffic.

And then there's Microsoft, which started with their homepage. This Potemkin village approach to a responsive redesign can frustrate users—promising them a website that works well on mobile devices, only to betray those expectations on the first tap. But Chris Balt from Microsoft reported that it helped them get organizational buy-in on going responsive:

> Other sites have taken different approaches, starting from the bottom up or with some out-of-the-way corner of the site. Our attempt to do it first with the homepage—and beautifully so, if I say so myself—was a good choice. It led to significant visibility that I don't think we would have gotten if we had started with some second-level support site or something like that. So even though the experience for a user may have suffered—they are one click away from a non-responsive experience—the visibility that it obtained us politically, organizationally, both inside and outside the company, made it a great choice. I am very glad that we did it that way (http://bkaprt.com/gr/01-14/).

Here's how you might go about rolling out a responsive redesign by section:

- **Choose a section** that reflects the types of problems or design patterns you'll find elsewhere on the site. Some sections, like "Investor Relations" or "About Us," may be easier to implement because they have relatively simple content and layouts—but they won't provide as much insight about how to handle more complex problems.

- **Focus on your core.** As with Pilates, your core does all the work. Look at your traffic and usage data to identify the pages and sections of the site that matter the most to users. Put your energy there.
- **Make sure your first-round stakeholders are on board** with the extra effort required to support the redesign. They'll be asked to make unfamiliar decisions—and they'll need to share and defend their rationale with the rest of the organization.
- **Track and document scope** to inform future initiatives. Knowing how long certain processes take, where design and development teams ran into difficulty, and which decisions were challenging for stakeholders will help you plan the next phase of work.
- **Make global decisions with everyone in mind.** Some choices really do affect everyone. Dealing with responsive images, designing navigation menus, identifying core content types, developing reusable modules as part of a design system— such topics require buy-in from more than just the people managing a particular page or section.

ORGANIZATIONAL CHANGE

You've made a plan for rolling out your responsive redesign, taking into account how your organization makes decisions. You've gotten buy-in on the budget and timeline, even though it may cost a little more than everyone hoped. You've communicated to stakeholders how their involvement may change, and you've done your best to prepare them for what might go wrong.

Have you planned to restructure your teams, change reporting relationships, or hire for new roles? Because you may need to do that, too.

Trei Brundrett, Chief Product Officer at Vox Media, said, "A responsive design approach really wasn't a design approach, it was an organizational approach to thinking and aligning everything else about how we worked and how we built things together." The process of going responsive forced Vox to go deeper into what it meant to have a collaborative culture (http://bkaprt.com/gr/02-09/).

Integrate your mobile team

When smartphones were new to the world, many companies set up a "mobile" team to research and evangelize this new platform. Members of these teams were encouraged—even incentivized—to develop solutions separate from the lumbering 500-pound gorilla that is the desktop website. Freed from the strictures of negotiating with dozens of stakeholders, teams were able to build native apps or m-dot sites quickly.

But what worked when mobile was a blip on the radar no longer works when mobile is 50% of your traffic. Teams now must be encouraged—and incentivized—to build products that work across all devices. A separate mobile team doesn't help you get there, as Bill Scott from PayPal found:

> *The way the company was organized really contributed to this problem. Mobile was a separate organization; thinking about and talking about mobile was another team's responsibility. So teams really didn't think about how to make experiences that just naturally span across platforms. The world was sharply divided between native and web, and web was just thought of as desktop (http://bkaprt.com/gr/01-52/).*

Remember that people whose jobs are defined by treating mobile as a distinct platform will have good reason to argue against responsive design. Many organizations privately report they had a tricky political situation to navigate, where responsive, app, and m-dot approaches stood as proxies for the professional future of leaders within the team. Mobile is yet another instance where the user experience should not mirror your organizational structure.

Integrate your designers and developers

Of all the planning involved in setting up a responsive redesign, perhaps none comes as a bigger surprise than the need to reorganize the design and development teams. Collaboration and iteration—always a good idea—are at the very heart of a successful responsive redesign. Processes built on prototyping require teams to work closely together. Designs can't simply be documented in comps or specs and then "thrown over the wall" to developers.

While it's tempting to think this problem can be solved on a short-term case-by-case basis—maybe by moving one developer's desk for a couple of months—the long-term success of responsive projects requires that your design and development teams all pull in the same direction. Tom Maslen, Tech Lead at the BBC, explained, "If you want to make better products, if you want faster development cycles, then embed UX into the development teams and make us jointly responsible for the same objective: a working website" (http://bkaprt.com/gr/02-10/). When designers and developers sit on different teams and report to different people, they're motivated by different goals and expectations. Aligning everyone may need to happen at higher levels of the org chart.

Even if design and development teams remain as separate groups, managers must train teams and facilitate a much higher degree of collaboration. Jason Chandler, Manager, Client Side Engineering at Expedia, explained that the need for his developers to work closely with the design team affected his hiring, training, and communication processes:

> *Some aspects of responsive design are quite complex. What we don't want is a hit-and-a-miss where no one can speak the same language, because that kills productivity. In order for this to work, it required really close integration between engineering and UX (http://bkaprt.com/gr/01-20/).*

You may also need to envision new roles with new skills. Fidelity created and started hiring for a new position called "UX developers." Nationwide created a new role called "creative technologist." Jason Grigsby of Cloud Four said they are hiring for a position they just created, titled "front-end designer." These new roles help bridge design and development processes.

We're building working prototypes now rather than creating documents, comps, and other static deliverables.

Train your technical team

Your core team—the designers and developers tasked with actually building the responsive design—need training on how to do it right. Even experienced development teams require time to get up to speed on new responsive design techniques. The basics of fluid grids, flexible images, and media queries are relatively straightforward—but it takes real-world experience to know how to deal with complex content challenges, manage testing across devices, and ensure fast performance on every platform.

Think about how you will train and educate your technical team:

- **What training do you plan to offer?** Conference or workshop sessions will deliver more value if multiple members of the team participate. Do you have a budget for books, webinars, or training videos? Plan to discuss or watch them together.
- **Do you plan to work with an outside agency to complete this work?** If so, build time for training your in-house staff into the scope of work—otherwise the agency team will walk out the door with all the experience.
- **Do you plan to task a small, centralized team with implementing the responsive design?** If that team will later be responsible for coaching other product teams on responsive rollouts, build time into the process for knowledge-sharing along the way. Expedia completed a responsive redesign of their cars section (a smaller, simpler line of business) in parallel with their hotels section (their bread and butter). The team that led these processes gained valuable insight that later benefited teams working on flights and vacation packages (http://bkaprt.com/gr/01-20/).
- **Do you need the entire organization to understand how responsive design changes the process?** (Yes, you do.) Responsive design will change the way you work and com-

municate, moving away from static comps and formal documentation. Project managers, backend developers, and QA testers need to work differently—even if they are not considered part of the "responsive redesign." Marriott implemented a distributed model that was designed to give *everyone* experience in designing and building responsive sites. Rather than tasking one centralized team to do the work, each individual group and business unit was responsible for making their own pages responsive. It took longer and was more complicated, but it was an approach to training that delivered the organizational transformation they needed (http://bkaprt.com/gr/01-53/).

Training is important, but there is no substitute for doing the work. Depending on how your company handles scoping and budgeting, you may want to break training costs out of the budget. Learning how to work in a new way is the real challenge.

LEVELING UP

What if I told you that a responsive redesign would, in the end, deliver more than a website that works on smartphones and tablets? As should be abundantly clear by now, responsive design is a learning experience as much as a concrete outcome.

Livia Labate from Marriott, in a personal conversation, described their responsive program as three initiatives in one:

1. **Create the responsive site**, so the website works across multiple devices.
2. **Train teams on new technical skills**, whether those are specific to responsive design, like media queries or responsive images, or more general, like prototyping.
3. **Adopt a new process** and a new set of values for the organization, like working in a more collaborative, iterative way.

Teams report that going responsive makes them more collaborative, and the benefits of that last beyond this one initiative. Frank Punzo, Interactive Design Manager at Children's Hospital of Philadelphia, said their redesign forced the design and content teams to work closely: "It's really benefited the team because it shows the way we all think and work together, and it's just made us more of a cohesive unit" (http://bkaprt.com/gr/02-11/).

This new reality gives teams a chance to be more strategic about how they approach the website, engaging designers and developers in conversations about the broader business value of their work. Robert Huddleston, Senior Creative Director of UX/UI at Capital One, said the success of their responsive design helped to shift company perception of their team and reinforce their value:

> We saw such a huge amount of business benefit from this responsive effort that it brought the design team to a place where we now have a seat at the table when we talk about business strategy. We deliver business value. We're not just a production team where we're cranking out web pages. We are influencers now when it comes to brand strategy and business strategy based on this one effort. It's really done a lot for our team internally (http://bkaprt.com/gr/01-39/).

Organizations gain value from responsive projects that goes well beyond a new website. One of the biggest benefits comes from a place you might not expect—a focus on performance. Let's look at how these changes in process and culture can help speed up your site.

3 SPEED UP YOUR SITE

" *The company wasn't merely doing a redesign, they were also starting down the path to a better culture of performance inside their organization.*"
—TIM KADLEC, "'RWD Is Bad for Performance' Is Good for Performance"
(http://bkaprt.com/gr/03-01/)

A FRIEND WHO READ a very early draft of this book said, "The order of the sections seems off. It should follow a typical design process, with performance coming later."

That's precisely the problem we're trying to solve.

After all the design decisions have been made and all the pages built, we discover that the website is too damn slow. Performance optimization is done in retrospect as a belated attempt to fix what's already broken. When you're going responsive, that doesn't work anymore.

Have you ever ignored your winter weight gain—reasoning that you still fit into your comfy pants—but then realized it was time to go on a diet once swimsuit season rolled around? Trying to fit a bloated desktop website into a slim-fitting mobile screen is a bit like that. Slower connection speeds and pay-by-the-megabyte downloads on mobile mean that, now, people are finally paying attention to performance problems.

Getting your company to care about performance may be one of the best outcomes of implementing a responsive design. When you make decisions about what to include on the website through the lens of performance, you're forced to make tough decisions about what *really* provides value to the user. And that results in a better experience for everyone.

A BRIEF PERFORMANCE PRIMER

How fast any given web page loads depends on many factors: the weight of code and content, the number of server calls, the relative speed of the network, and the capabilities of the browser and the device—just to name a few. Because performance is so technical, conversations about how to improve it are typically left to engineers. This needs to change. Designers, marketers, and stakeholders must understand how their decisions will affect the speed of the website, and how tradeoffs will be negotiated.

Although performance optimization is complicated, most team members only need to understand the basics, which I'll cover here. (For a closer look, pick up a copy of *Designing for Performance* by Lara Hogan and *Responsible Responsive Design* by Scott Jehl.)

Page weight

Statistics from the HTTP Archive Report, analyzing traffic from 300,000 websites, show that the average web page in 2014 weighed around 2 MB (1.953 MB, to be precise), which reflects an increase of 15% from 2013 (http://bkaprt.com/gr/03-02/). The size of the average web page has increased 186% since 2010 (http://bkaprt.com/gr/03-03/). As Jason Grigsby said, "We've remade the Internet in our own image, which, in the United States, is obese" (http://bkaprt.com/gr/03-04/).

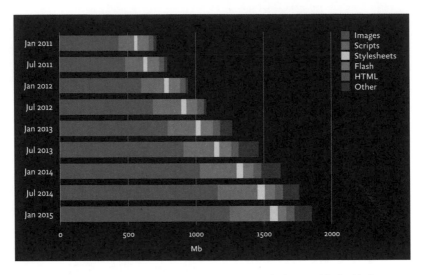

FIG 3.1: Data from the HTTP Archive shows that page weight has roughly doubled over the past few years (http://bkaprt.com/gr/03-05/).

Images make up the largest percentage of page weight—more than 50% on average. Web fonts are another growing factor, shown in "other." Developers can optimize file size, especially for CSS and HTML, but doing so doesn't deliver enough performance gains to offset other increases (**FIG 3.1**).

Server calls

Every element on a web page—HTML, CSS, images, fonts— requires the browser to make a request from the web server. Sometimes those requests get redirected to a different server, like when the user gets sent over to a different domain or an object is downloaded from a third-party server. All of these requests and redirects take time to receive and process.

While we can reduce the number of elements on the page and bundle multiple files so they can be downloaded in one server call, much of the delay is based on how far away the user is from the server itself. This delay varies widely and may add anywhere from 100 milliseconds for a fast wired connection to a full two seconds (or more) over mobile networks.

Stakeholders don't need to worry too much about the nuts and bolts of server calls, except to be aware that it isn't entirely an engineering problem. Redirects and third-party server calls have a real effect on performance and your entire team should take this into account when making decisions.

Download speed

So, how fast does the page load? While that seems like the metric we should focus on, many factors influence how quickly a page loads for any given user—including device type and network speed—and not all of them are within our control. Experts in web performance frame goals for download speed under specific network conditions (like 3G or broadband) and evaluate performance at certain percentiles (like the best, average, and worst download times—or first, fiftieth, and ninety-ninth percentiles).

Perceived performance

"Time to interact" is a metric that evaluates the perceived performance of the site—how quickly the page appears to load. How fast a user *thinks* the site loads is more important than how fast it really loads. Developers use a variety of techniques to influence users' perception of response time—like setting active states for buttons, using momentum scrolling, and choosing to display spinners and progress bars (or avoiding them).

But the biggest effect on perceived performance doesn't come from these little interface tricks. A study by User Interface Engineering found that Amazon, the slowest site in the study, was perceived to be one of the fastest, while About.com, despite being the fastest to download, was rated slowest by users. What caused these paradoxical results? It turns out there is a strong correlation between perceived performance and being able to complete tasks (http://bkaprt.com/gr/03-06/).

Good coding practices can make sites feel faster by loading the most important information first. Users can start reading or interacting with the site immediately while the rest of the page continues to load. Of course, that means you'll need to understand the priority of each element on the page. Better performance requires more than attention from developers— it needs insight from UX designers, marketers, and content strategists, too.

WHY PERFORMANCE MATTERS

Your design decisions doom your users to staring at their phones, waiting impatiently for your site to load—or send them into the alluring embrace of your competitors. Instead of waiting until the site is built and launched to figure this out, get your whole team focused on performance from the start.

Nobody cares about speed for its own sake—they care about the value a faster website provides to the business and the user. So start talking about why making decisions through the lens of performance will change the way you design. A culture of performance means framing design decisions and content choices as tradeoffs that ultimately affect the user experience and the bottom line.

Interactivity

Delays in response time have a cognitive cost. Does the user's attention wander? Does she feel in control? That hinges on how quickly the device appears to respond.

Performance requirements are based on fundamental aspects of human cognition and perception—they don't change with the technology. Eye tracking research on web users today shows the same findings as human factors research on mainframe users from forty years ago: users notice and are affected by sluggish response times, even those under one second (http://bkaprt.com/gr/03-07/).

Jakob Nielsen, called "The Guru of Web Page Usability" by the *New York Times,* has been writing about web performance and response times since 1993. His findings—consistent over the past twenty years—show that even the tiniest delays change how users interact with websites (http://bkaprt.com/gr/03-08/):

- **100 milliseconds.** For a web application that requires instantaneous feedback—say, when objects are selected or dragged—response times must be under 100 milliseconds. (Yes, that's one-tenth of a second!) Longer waits mean that the experience feels sluggish.
- **1 second.** For a website that the user expects to read and navigate, response times should be under one second. Longer waits mean that users lose their sense of "flow" and feel like they're waiting for the device to respond. With a delay of a second or two, users must really want to use the website—otherwise, they lose focus.
- **10 seconds.** For all interactions, response times must be under ten seconds. Longer waits mean that users will switch to another task, and need to reorient themselves when they return—which is a productivity-killer. A delay of ten seconds means users are likely to give up on the website.

What happens after even a short delay? Users abandon the site outright, or they muddle onward, but conversion rates are low.

Abandonment

When a page loads slowly, many users leave and don't come back. "Bounce rate" is one of the most important metrics we can use to analyze web and mobile performance (**FIG 3.2**).

By reviewing abandonment data across more than 150 websites and 150 million page views, Gomez, cited by eConsultancy, found that an increase in response time from two to ten seconds increased abandonment rates by 38% (http://bkaprt.com/gr/03-09/).

Similarly, research from Aberdeen found that 25% of users will abandon a web application after just three seconds of delay (http://bkaprt.com/gr/03-10/, PDF, requires registration).

Etsy found that adding 160 KB of images to a page increased bounce rate by 12% on mobile devices, according to Lara Hogan, author of *Designing for Performance* (http://bkaprt.com/gr/03-11/).

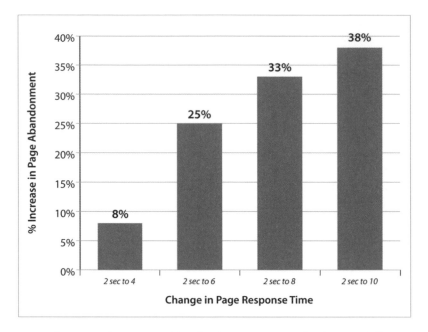

FIG 3.2: Bounce rate increases precipitously when page response time increases. When load times are between six and ten seconds, you can expect a sizable number of users to abandon immediately.

SEO

Google has used site speed in its ranking algorithm since 2010 (http://bkaprt.com/gr/03-12/). Although speed is not as important as page relevance, it does matter. Google penalizes common mobile configuration problems that affect site performance, like faulty redirects (http://bkaprt.com/gr/03-13/). Google seems to be experimenting with a "slow" label for websites, a sort of Scarlet Letter for sites that don't perform well (http://bkaprt.com/gr/03-13/). Whatever happens with this experiment, it's clear that Google takes performance seriously and will rank sites lower if they're too slow.

Conversion rate

Conversion rates on smartphones are already quite low. Customers are more likely to use their phones for research, then purchase in another channel—on their desktop, or potentially in-store. Research from Monetate, cited by Smart Insights, found that conversion rates on smartphones are generally under 1% (**FIG 3.3**). Conversion rates on tablet devices are similar to desktop computers (http://bkaprt.com/gr/03-15/).

Increasing conversions requires attention to many different factors, but one clear-cut way to improve conversion rates is improving site speed (**FIG 3.4**). Research by Gomez, cited by Compuware, of more than thirty major retailers found that conversion rates increased 74% when page-load time dropped from eight seconds to two seconds (http://bkaprt.com/gr/03-16/, PDF).

Similar conversion rate gains have been found by many other firms that have invested in improving web performance—while increasing revenue for retailers is the most obvious scenario, firms that measure conversion by downloads or donations also have seen a boost. Paying attention to performance directly translates into increased business value.

- **Walmart.** By acknowledging that they weren't the fastest retailer on the web, Walmart was able to focus on improving load times (**FIG 3.5**). For every second of improvement, they experienced up to a 2% increase in conversions; for every 100 milliseconds of improvement, they grew incremental revenue by up to 1% (http://bkaprt.com/gr/03-17/).
- **GQ.** The magazine reduced page load time 80% (down to two seconds), and saw an 80% increase in monthly unique visitors, from 6 million to 11 million. Median time spent on site increased from 5.9 minutes to 7.8 minutes (http://bkaprt.com/gr/03-18/.
- **Google and Bing.** The two leading search engines A/B tested performance and found that a 500-millisecond delay caused a 20% drop in traffic (http://bkaprt.com/gr/03-19/).
- **Staples.** By reducing the median homepage download time by one second (and a whopping six seconds for visitors in the ninety-eighth percentile), Staples increased their conversion rate by 10% (http://bkaprt.com/gr/03-20/).

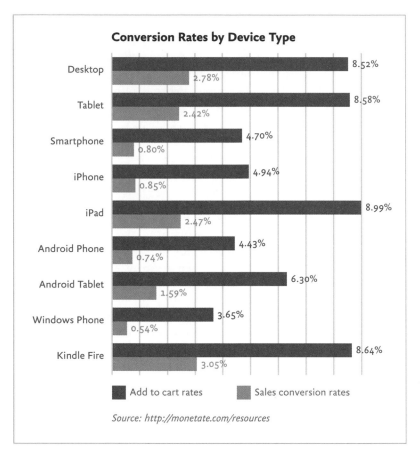

FIG 3.3: No matter what type of smartphone people have, they don't really use them to transact.

- **Firefox.** By taking 2.2 seconds off the average page load time, Firefox increased download conversions by 15.4% (http://bkaprt.com/gr/03-21/).
- **Shopzilla.** The retailer reduced page load time by five seconds and increased site conversion rates between 7 to 12% (http://bkaprt.com/gr/03-22/).

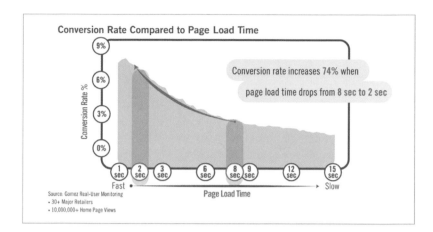

FIG 3.4: Remember when we said that pages should load within one or two seconds? Here's why.

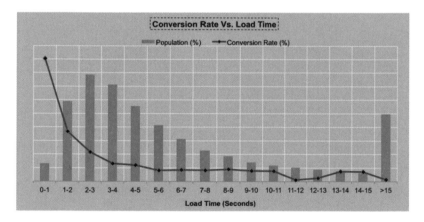

FIG 3.5: Walmart shared data that showed conversion rate dropped off significantly after just one second, even though the majority of their customers saw much longer load times.

- **Obama for America.** The 2012 campaign website improved page load time from five seconds to two seconds. After conducting 240 A/B tests, the new site improved donation conversions by 14%, an increase of over $34 million (http://bkaprt.com/gr/03-23/).

RESPONSIVE AND PERFORMANCE

Responsive design has developed a reputation for being "bad for performance." Even advocates for responsive design conclude that it incurs performance tradeoffs that could be avoided by maintaining separate desktop and m-dot websites. Guy Podjarny, formerly CTO, Web and Mobile at Akamai, wrote, "I think you have to face the music—RWD makes it very hard to write a fast website" (http://bkaprt.com/gr/03-24/). He went on to say that even though he would recommend responsive design to most organizations, it "puts some real roadblocks in the way of a website trying to be fast."

Let's look at two things that slow down responsive websites.

Complex front-end code

The HTML and CSS for responsive sites is, by definition, more complex than standalone desktop or mobile sites. Apples to apples, even the most carefully built responsive website will be slightly larger and require more processing—and that's the best-case scenario. In an ideal world, everyone would be experts in planning and building sites using progressive enhancement, so each device would only download the code that it needs. In the real world, responsive designs are sometimes flawed, built by inexperienced developers working under tight deadlines—so users wind up downloading CSS or scripts they don't need.

But HTML, CSS, and scripts make up a small fraction of the total page weight. The real problem occurs when imperfectly implemented responsive design forces less-capable devices to download *content* that doesn't get shown to the user.

Overdownloading content

Guy Podjarny conducted studies of responsive web design performance in 2012 and 2013. The second study found that 72% of responsive websites download the full content of the website at every resolution, while only 6% of sites are significantly lighter at smaller screen sizes (http://bkaprt.com/gr/03-25/).

The primary causes of overdownloading are techniques used to maintain the experience for desktop users at the expense of mobile users:

- **Download and hide.** The simplest way to preserve the desktop experience without overwhelming mobile users is to hide content on smaller screens. Sidebars, large images, or anything built in Flash gets set to `display:none` at smaller breakpoints. Mobile devices still load all of the content (possibly over slower, pay-by-the-megabyte cellular networks), but it doesn't get shown to the user. The user pays the price in slower speeds and receives no benefit from downloading all that content.
- **Download and shrink.** Large images or other media types are downloaded and then scaled for smaller devices, which means the less-capable devices pay the penalty for all that high-bandwidth media.

Some of the problems with overdownloading can be solved by improving the quality of responsive design implementations—something that will emerge as developers get more practice. Tim Kadlec, author of *Implementing Responsive Design* says, "Blame the implementation, not the technique" (http://bkaprt. com/gr/03-26/). Rather than downloading and shrinking large images, optimize your image files or implement responsive images. Rather than downloading and hiding content, make sure less capable devices only download what they need.

PERFORMANCE IS A CONTENT STRATEGY PROBLEM

Your developers are likely doing everything in their power to fix your performance problems. They're refactoring CSS and JavaScript, combining files to reduce the number of server calls, compressing or caching files and images—even removing unnecessary spaces in code, a process called "minification."

FIG 3.6: No, the desktop site is not going to "look too empty" if you clean up and pare down your content for mobile. That is the least of your concerns.

What are *you* doing?

The biggest culprits behind bloated, heavy pages aren't necessarily under your developers' control. Performance suffers because stakeholders insist they must have everything but the kitchen sink on the website. Full-bleed images, giant carousels, web fonts, social widgets—each of these comes at a cost, and the user pays for it in download speed.

Unnecessary content

Too often, companies focus on making small performance improvements when the real benefits would come from making difficult decisions about what needs to be on the website. It's a bit like going to the Container Store to buy yet another plastic organizer, when what you need to do is to throw things away.

One of the most common concerns I hear from companies about going responsive is this: "But won't the desktop look empty?" Your homepage weighs 7MB. Your right column is a junk drawer. Your nav goes five levels deep. Your problem is not that your website will be too spartan (**FIG 3.6**).

Be honest: are you keeping everything on your website because you know it's providing value? Or because you don't want to have all the conversations you know you'd need to have with stakeholders to remove it? It's not okay to hide content from mobile users or develop an m-dot site that offers a subset of what's on the "real" website. But it is okay—necessary, even—to clean up the clutter. In Chapter 4, we'll cover how to evaluate content quality, but first let's look at some of the types of content that slow down websites.

Large images

While images are a major contributor to page weight even on desktop sites, they're a particular problem for responsive sites, because different device sizes and screen resolutions may require different image sizes or entirely different image crops. Tim Kadlec wrote, "The most common offender for poor responsive performance is downloading unnecessarily large images, or worse yet, multiple sizes of the same image" (http://bkaprt.com/gr/03-27/). (For more about responsive images, check out the Resources in the back of the book.)

While developers have all sorts of techniques to optimize images, the first line of defense should be to ask yourself: do we need this image at all? Images are often merely decorative, advocated by designers or marketers who like the layout but haven't considered the performance tradeoffs.

Mobile is a great test of whether stakeholders *really* need those giant images. If your team thinks it's okay to remove an image from the smartphone view, then maybe no one really needs it at all.

Carousels

So, you've got some large images, and you wonder, "How can I pack the biggest performance hit into the smallest amount of space?" A carousel may be for you.

Marketers and stakeholders *love* carousels. Rather than make tough decisions about how to allocate precious real estate, people shove everything into a rotator and call it a day. Trouble

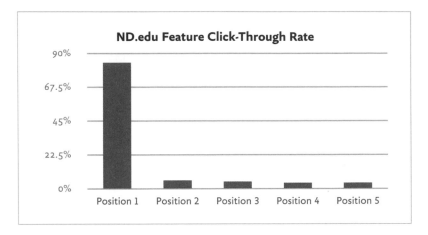

FIG 3.7: Of the 1% of visitors to the Notre Dame website who interacted with a carousel, 84% visited the first position in the rotator. Each subsequent position garnered only about 4% of the views.

is, that doesn't actually solve the problem—users don't click through the images in the carousel, but downloading all those files can drag down performance (**FIG 3.7**). Erik Runyon, Technical Director at Notre Dame University, reported data from several websites showing few users interact with carousels beyond the first position in the rotator (http://bkaprt.com/gr/03-28/).

Alas, it's likely that carousels will be an even more popular design pattern on mobile devices, because screen real estate is even more constrained. *Stop it.* Think of it this way: users must swipe to get to the content—swiping horizontally in a carousel or vertically on the page. But users are *less* likely to see and interact with the items in a carousel! A carousel adds unnecessary code and page weight to achieve this flawed objective.

Web fonts

Remember the days when every single website used a combination of Arial and Georgia? A small number of fonts were available on every platform, and using them guaranteed that web pages looked the way designers intended.

In our fragmented mobile device landscape, we can't assume every user will have the same system fonts anymore. In his research to create a compatibility table of default fonts across major operating systems, Jordan Moore, Web Designer and Front-end Developer at Eyekiller, was forced to conclude: "There is no safe native typographic foundation on today's web" (http://bkaprt.com/gr/03-29/).

Fortunately, today we have web fonts. Web fonts help maintain brand consistency across platforms—but they also require the user to download more files, and that affects performance. Poorly implemented web fonts also hurt perceived performance, blocking screen rendering while they load or displaying a flash of unstyled text. While there are plenty of tricks developers can use to manage the way fonts get loaded, marketers and designers should do their part, too, by making decisions about which fonts are absolutely, positively required. Ask yourself:

- **Do we need all these fonts?** Ransom-note typography has been popular since the desktop publishing era, but just because you can doesn't mean you should.
- **Do we need every weight and character set for this font?** Font families are broken down by weight and style. If the bold italic version of the font isn't needed, for example, protect your site performance by not including it.
- **Could we choose a different typeface?** Because fonts must be loaded on every page, the file size for the font itself really matters. Katie Kovalcin, Designer at Sparkbox, suggests choosing an alternative typeface with a similar style and smaller file size (http://bkaprt.com/gr/03-30/).
- **Do smaller screens need to look exactly like larger screens?** It's possible to compromise by sending custom fonts only to larger screens—but everyone needs to agree on making that tradeoff (http://bkaprt.com/gr/03-31/).
- **Could we replace icon fonts with SVG?** Many sites have tried to improve performance by replacing images with icon fonts. But icon fonts pose an accessibility problem for peo-

ple using screen readers or special system fonts for dyslexia (http://bkaprt.com/gr/03-32/). SVG (scalable vector graphics) is a more accessible, lightweight solution.

Social tools

Facebook! Twitter! Tumblr! Pinterest! Better add LinkedIn, Google+, Reddit! Pretty soon the share icon lists thirty-six potential places where someone could share your web page. Asking the marketing team to remove a few of the less popular sites is usually met with dismay. "But what about Snapchat?" they ask.

Social media widgets can cause slow or janky page loading. You might look at those tiny social icons and wonder how something so small can be so heavy. Calling out to all those external domains, using analytics software to track the number of clicks on each—it adds up (http://bkaprt.com/gr/03-33/). As with everything related to performance, smart developers can control how and when these widgets load, in an effort to improve perceived performance.

Your job is to communicate that adding social networks isn't free. Ask yourself:

- **Do you need share functionality at all?** I see these hopeful share buttons on web pages that advertise girdles and hemorrhoid cream, and wonder if marketers thought through any realistic scenarios where a person would share that on Facebook. Smashing Magazine removed Facebook buttons and reported their traffic from Facebook *increased*, because readers shared articles rather than simply liking them (http://bkaprt.com/gr/03-34/).
- **Would a link suffice?** A case can be made that share icons offer an important visual reminder, and share widgets offer additional functionality (like adding followers on Facebook, or improving SEO with Google+). But if the goal is simply to enable sharing, a link requires less code.
- **Do you need every social network on the planet?** Maybe just stick with a few top sites or the ones most relevant for your audience.

Third-party services

All third-party tools can affect performance. Social tools are likely culprits, because what looks like a simple widget can involve dozens of calls to external sites. But any embedded third-party service will hurt performance—recommendations engines, analytics, maps, videos, even (especially!) advertising. Perry Hewitt, Chief Digital Officer at Harvard University, said that these services can hurt performance if developers don't carefully plan how pages will render so they feel speedy:

> We look at load time and at people's perception of load time, too. Sometimes the numbers come back larger than we'd like, and we realize it's the third-party services at the bottom of the page that are not really affecting the core user experience. We want to optimize for the most responsible numbers, and have a clear understanding of how the weight is affecting user experience (http://bkaprt.com/gr/03-35/).

Even scarier—some third-party services send out a cascade of server calls to *fourth parties*. Like those "friends of friends" who show up for your barbecue at 3 a.m., fourth-party services are completely out of your control (http://bkaprt.com/gr/03-36/).

Why do you have third-party services in the first place? In many cases, it's because you believe that business value—increased conversions—will accrue from the functionality the service provides. But slower page loading comes at a cost—fewer users means fewer conversions. Time for a cost-benefit analysis (http://bkaprt.com/gr/03-37/):

- **What conversion rate increase do you expect to achieve?** The vendor should be able to provide the average increase you can expect when adding the service.
- **What performance decrease will you incur?** A simple A/B test comparing your site with and without the third-party service should give you that number.
- **What conversion rate decrease will you incur due to slower performance?** This number can be difficult to compute, but

a 7% loss in conversions for every additional one-second delay is an established metric (http://bkaprt.com/gr/03-38/).

Even though many third-party services promise fantastic conversion rate increases with "only one line of JavaScript!" the reality is that they slow your site down. If the increased conversion rate sounds too good to be true, it just might be.

Make sure users can get to the content they want first, and load third-party services last so they don't affect perceived performance (http://bkaprt.com/gr/03-39/).

SETTING A PERFORMANCE BUDGET

Building a culture of performance sounds great—in theory. But anyone who's ever sat in a design review with a team of stakeholders, each one making an impassioned plea for their "thing," knows that managing performance throughout the design and development process can be death by a thousand paper cuts.

You can't manage what you don't measure, right? Mark Perkins, Senior Front-End Developer at Clearleft, first proposed the idea of setting a performance budget. By getting stakeholders to agree upfront that each page should not weigh more than, say, 1 MB, performance tradeoffs due to design and development decisions become more tangible:

> *The important point is to look at every decision, right through the design/build process, as something that has consequence. Having a pre-defined "budget" is a clear, tangible way to frame decisions about what can and can't be included, and at a suitably early stage in the project (http://bkaprt.com/gr/03-40/).*

Developers responsible for performance might jump in here and argue that the causes of poor performance go well beyond simple metrics like page weight—and that's true. But the goal of setting a performance budget isn't to mirror the exact performance metrics for the website—it's to give stakeholders a way to focus on the aspects of performance that are within their control.

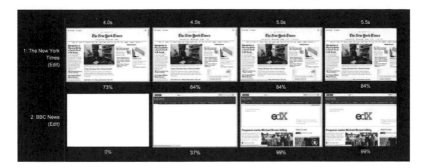

FIG 3.8: WebPagetest provides a filmstrip view showing how much of the page has rendered over time.

When setting a performance budget, consider the following:

- **Current page weight.** Your maximum budget for page weight should be achievable, so define your goal by taking into account where you are today. What is the average page weight across your entire site? What about some of your heaviest pages, perhaps the homepage or a complex product page? You'll want to set aggressive but realistic goals.
- **Competitive evaluation.** Your budget should also look at where you are in relation to your competitors. Some stakeholders won't bat an eyelash at a page weight budget, but will be immediately motivated to change by looking at faster competitors (**FIG 3.8**). WebPagetest is an open-source comparison tool that evaluates multiple URLs and outputs a filmstrip showing how the pages render (http://bkaprt.com/gr/03-41/).
- **Server calls.** While the number of round-trips is not necessarily in the hands of your stakeholders, they should be aware of the effect of adding resources or third-party server calls to each page. Consider setting a budget for these resources, too. (Since each web font requires a third-party server call, many teams find it helpful to set a specific budget for the number of fonts that can be used.)
- **Experience metrics.** While metrics like *total load time* or *time to first interaction* aren't directly in your stakeholders' control,

communicating your goals for these metrics can help frame the discussion.

- **Custom load metrics.** Beyond general experience metrics like time to interact, many companies define custom metrics to evaluate performance. Twitter notably measures *time to first Tweet*, defined as the amount of time from clicking a link to viewing the first Tweet on each page's timeline (http://bkaprt.com/gr/03-42/). Steve Souders from Speed-Curve described developing custom metrics to evaluate hero image rendering (http://bkaprt.com/gr/03-43/).

Sharing data about the effect of performance on business metrics like conversion rate will put the performance discussion in terms your stakeholders care about. Jason Thibeault, Senior Director of Marketing Strategy at Limelight Networks, told Forrester Research:

> *It's a matter of translation. If you're speaking to IT, time-to-first-render and time-to-first-interaction are the metrics to focus on. If you're speaking to marketing, then focus on conversions and bounce rates (http://bkaprt.com/gr/03-44/, PDF, requires purchase).*

Remember: the goal of setting a performance budget isn't to have stakeholders use the same metrics as developers—it's to get the entire team focused on performance.

We've talked about how unnecessary content can slow down your site. But cleaning up content provides benefits that go beyond improving performance. Let's look at some of the ways a responsive project can make a site easier to read and navigate by offering information that users *really* need.

4 CLEAN UP YOUR CONTENT

" *"The responsive design became a content solution and not just a technical solution to make the ongoing evolution of our digital products more robust."*
—**ALEX BREUER**, The Guardian (http://bkaprt.com/gr/02-08/)

FLUID GRIDS, flexible images, and media queries: nothing in the definition of responsive web design says anything about your content. And yet, a lasting benefit for many organizations comes from the process of cleaning up and paring down content.

It probably comes as no surprise that creating a good user experience across all devices means presenting less content, better content, and more thoughtfully prioritized content. Gone are the days when we could assume that users want (and look at) everything we cram onto the page and shove into the right column. Truth is, users *never* wanted all that dreck. Now, with smaller screens, we're forced to acknowledge that uncomfortable truth and make decisions about what *really* matters.

Companies that show their "corporate underpants" by reflecting their organizational structure in their navigation will struggle to make the right choices, because decisions will still be grounded in stakeholder power structures rather than in customer needs. Companies that want to implement a genuinely user-centered approach will find a responsive redesign to be one of the best opportunities to do so.

The techniques for prioritizing, editing, and structuring content aren't new—content strategists and user experience designers have long advocated for a more thoughtful approach to how content gets created, managed, and maintained. But content is time-consuming to edit and may require a lengthy review process. In light of other, competing priorities, cleaning up content often winds up at the bottom of the list.

I often describe mobile as a trojan horse that gives teams access to senior decision-makers and the power to make changes to content that might previously have been unattainable. Saying "you need to fix your editorial workflow" or "you need structured content" may not get the CEO's attention—but saying "if you want your mobile website to succeed, you need to make these changes" may be just the argument that finally resonates.

Every responsive design project is also a content strategy project. Let's look at how common content strategy processes can help you when you're building a website that serves all devices.

EDITORIAL PROCESSES

Like the stars of an episode of *Hoarders,* most companies suffer from an inability to let anything go. Team members feel daunted by the effort required to sift through the garbage piled in every corner of the page. It's easier to use a giant shovel to dump the old content into new designs.

Teams that try this approach when implementing a responsive retrofit quickly find that they can't avoid the content problem forever. Rob Huddleston from Capital One said that seeing the new responsive website was what finally made stakeholders realize they needed a new approach to content strategy:

One thing that the retrofit did (not changing the desktop) was shine a big bright light on the content issues. People saw their content on a smaller device, saw what an overabundance of content there was and how unnecessary it was. Finally—it took a year—but we finally have business partners saying, "Okay, you were right, we need to think content first. Let's redesign our site" (http://bkaprt.com/gr/01-39/).

Whether you're cleaning up content after a responsive retrofit or proactively editing and structuring content to inform the design process, it's time to take out the trash.

Inventory and audit

Content strategists encourage starting with an inventory and audit of your content, and for good reason—you need to know what you're working with to make informed decisions.

An inventory is an objective document that captures the facts about your content: what it's called, when it was created, who owns it, and how big it is. It may also capture analytics data or information from search logs, which is especially useful as you move into the auditing stage. An audit is a subjective process in which you evaluate whether the content provides value and make choices about how to deal with it by editing it, deleting it altogether, or keeping it on the site as-is. (A complete guide to conducting an inventory and audit of your content is outside the scope of this book, but I cover the process in detail in *Content Strategy for Mobile*.)

One challenge with auditing and inventorying content to support a responsive design is that teams must gather more granular data. While typical content strategy processes focus on the *page* level, you'll need to drill down to the module or chunk level to prioritize and structure your content. You'll need to identify character or word counts for headlines, teasers, and body copy. You may also need to inventory image sizes and crop ratios. Understanding content at this level of granularity takes longer and requires more effort than simply shoving pages around, but it will help you make informed design decisions.

Edit and restructure

While your design and development team is busy working through layouts and design patterns, writers and stakeholders can rewrite and reorganize the content. This editorial process can be one of the largest and most complex efforts in a responsive redesign, and often requires the following:

- hiring and managing teams of freelancers (hiring 10-20 copywriters in addition to full-time staff is not unheard of)
- training extended teams on appropriate style, voice and tone, and editorial practices
- reviewing content with subject matter experts, stakeholders, and legal or compliance teams
- migrating content from the current website into editing tools and prototypes, and then into the publishing system

I won't gloss over the challenge of planning this work: even with careful processes and enough resources, it will take longer than you expect. Suzanne Connaughton, Web Strategy and Operations Manager at Children's Hospital of Philadelphia, said they budgeted a year to revise their content, adding, "I feel like we still should have started earlier" (http://bkaprt.com/gr/ 02-12/). Justin McDowell, Web Designer at The Evergreen State College, said they thought their responsive redesign would be finished in July 2014, and as of April 2015 said:

> We are still working and we're maybe halfway through because we want to make sure that the web pages are as good as they can be, and a lot of that has to do with retooling the content (http://bkaprt.com/gr/04-01/).

Consider a section-by-section staged rollout if you fear that fixing all your content will prevent the site from launching. (Revisit Chapter 2 for more information about planning your rollout strategy.) Be honest with yourself about the level of effort required for a massive content remediation project—but don't underestimate the value you'll receive from doing it.

When the time comes to begin rewriting content, you can make your team's life easier (and get the job done more quickly) by using digital writing and editing tools.

Use digital content tools

Designers have learned to use new tools and workflows as they adjust to the fluidity of responsive design. Rather than relying on fixed Photoshop comps, they evolve new ways to design and prototype. Writers and content reviewers must do the same.

"You will pry Microsoft Word from my cold, dead hands." Even if content creators don't tell me that directly, I can see it in their eyes. It's like they have Stockholm Syndrome and have started identifying with their captors from the Microsoft Office suite of enterprise software.

Much like Photoshop does for design, Word and Excel constrain writers to an offline, print-centric model. Looking at real content in a prototype or publishing it on the web requires copying-and-pasting across multiple systems, often resulting in errors or version control problems. If writers expect to participate in an iterative design process, they must embrace digital tools.

Applications like Gather Content (http://bkaprt.com/gr/04-02/) and Draft (http://bkaprt.com/gr/04-03/) provide true digital writing and editing workflows. Even Google Docs offers a digital-first approach, without requiring a huge learning curve compared to Microsoft Word. Children's Hospital of Philadelphia opted to do most of their writing and editing in an instance of their new Drupal CMS, which gave their content team on-the-job training and the chance to provide feedback on the author experience (http://bkaprt.com/gr/02-12/). The value in using these tools comes from a combination of flexibility and constraints:

- **Limited styles.** If you've ever tried to copy and paste from Microsoft Word into your CMS, you know it passes along a ton of garbage formatting that needs to be stripped out, especially when authors add their own formatting rather than using style sheets (like specifying 14pt Times New Roman

Bold instead of `<h2>`.) If writers follow pre-defined styles (or better yet, use Markdown), designers and developers don't waste time stripping and reformatting text as it moves between systems.

- **Structured content.** Content strategists often provide content templates in Word or Excel to guide content creators (http://bkaprt.com/gr/04-04/). Even better would be to use a digital authoring environment. Content creators can be given basic forms to complete with editorial guidelines inline. Structured content constrains and guides authors, and makes moving the content into the CMS easier.
- **Collaboration and version control.** Online tools offer commenting and version control. Sure, everyone is comfortable using Track Changes in Word, but features like Suggesting mode in Google Docs provide an audit trail to show when and how changes were resolved.
- **APIs.** Want a trump card to play to argue against Word and Excel? Online tools have APIs that allow developers to pull content from one system to another. Want to see the most recent version of content in a prototype, or automatically migrate it into your CMS? Microsoft Word can't do that, but web-based tools like Google Docs can.

Less is more

Cleaning up and paring down content can massively reduce the number of pages on your site—a 75% reduction is not out of the question. Scott Childs, Experience Design Lead at Capital One, said that their responsive redesign was the tipping point that made stakeholders see the value of offering less (but better) content:

> We're working on projects right now where different business units are redesigning their entire section of the site. We're seeing page reductions of 60 to 70%. People are being really thoughtful about how we can get the most value out of content that is streamlined as much as possible (http://bkaprt.com/gr/01-39/).

Mike Donahue from Citrix consistently emphasized the value of starting with content, not with design, and said that aligning teams around a shared strategy for mobile content was what helped them focus:

In our benefits section alone, we managed to cut 215 pages of content down to about twenty, because we sat with the HR team and we co-developed and co-created their content with them. When you can get people aligned on goals and strategies, you can have these open conversations and really whittle things down to just what you truly need (http://bkaprt.com/gr/01-19/).

Now, having fewer pages isn't valuable for its own sake. The benefits come from a better user experience and reduced maintenance costs:

- **Improved navigation.** Fewer pages mean fewer levels of site navigation, which means it's easier to browse and find what you're looking for. Small screens are limited on space, but everyone benefits from simple navigation.
- **Easier to read.** The purpose and intent of each page becomes clear, as every element has to earn its keep.
- **Reduced costs.** Translation and content management costs add up. Mike Donahue from Citrix added, "There was some plain ol' bottom dollar ROI to us getting better at doing the content" (http://bkaprt.com/gr/01-19/).

When you have less content, it's easier to make sure valuable information gets seen. Prioritization exercises can help the team focus on what's most important.

CONTENT PRIORITIZATION

"Mobile first" has become such a buzzword that its definition has expanded to mean very different things to different people. At its core, mobile-first means using the constraints of a smaller, less-capable device to identify what matters most on each screen.

Perhaps the most valuable exercise for planning a content strategy and responsive redesign is a forced prioritization of objects on the page. This exercise is mobile-first made tangible. To make content and functionality work on the smallest screen sizes and least capable devices, stakeholders must make tough choices about what to keep and what to jettison. It's best to do this in a work session—at least in the initial stages. Remember, every website redesign must include at least one brainstorming exercise where you move some Post-it notes around on the wall.

Preparation

Get ready for your prioritization work session by identifying the pages and page elements you plan to discuss:

Understand user needs

This may sound painfully obvious, but you should know what users want and are looking for on your website before you come to the meeting. The books written about understanding user personas, goals, and tasks would fill a few library shelves, so if you're still not sure how to make sense of user needs, now is the time to start. User research and analytics data should give you a working understanding of which content and features users find most valuable. A journey mapping exercise may be valuable to understand common user flows. Plan to share this data with your team during the session if they're not familiar with it.

Select pages for discussion

You won't be able to review every page on the website in a work session, so pick a subset of pages in advance. Make a list of high-value pages you'd like to discuss with your team: the homepage, key landing pages, product pages, most popular pages, or pages with complex layouts. Simple structures (like article pages) are relatively straightforward to prioritize, while landing pages that serve as a jumping-off point often require more discussion because they're fraught with stakeholder politics. You'll probably only be able to look at two or three pages in a work session, so focus on the ones that are most difficult, most read, and most valuable.

Identify content modules

For each page, list the content modules you plan to discuss in advance and document them in a spreadsheet for reference during the meeting. Unless you're working only with team members responsible for content modeling and information architecture, it's easiest to do this before your work session—that way you won't spend the entire meeting debating how granular to make your modules and what to name them (FIG 4.1).

In the work session

A prioritization work session can be a fun way to get team members talking about which elements on the page are most important to the customer. It can also be a frustrating exercise for people who've never had to make hard choices. Brian Greene, Creative Technologist at Nationwide, said stakeholders struggled with prioritizing elements on the screen:

> *A forced prioritization is a challenge for some of our business partners because they're so used to saying, "Contact us and log in are at the same level of importance." We would force them: "No, you cannot do that. We need a number one, number two, number three"* (http://bkaprt.com/gr/04-05/).

Rank the modules

Start the exercise by asking stakeholders to state in one sentence what the purpose of each page is. For some pages—like a product page—it should be obvious that the goal is to research or purchase the product. For others, it will quickly become clear that stakeholders have wildly competing interpretations of

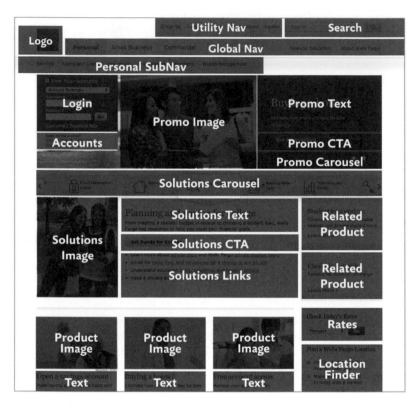

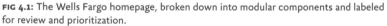

FIG 4.1: The Wells Fargo homepage, broken down into modular components and labeled for review and prioritization.

what the page is good for, or that no one understands its value to the user (FIG 4.2).

Next, ask team members to physically order each element to reflect the purpose of the page. A few options for how to conduct this exercise:

- **Arrange Post-it notes** labeled with the name of each module into a single stack column—no cheating by putting two Post-its side by side! This approach closely mimics the form

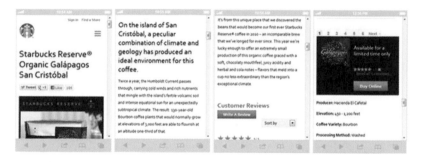

FIG 4.2: The first responsive version of the Starbucks website forced the visitor to scroll through several screens of product description and customer reviews to find the Buy button (http://bkaprt.com/gr/04-06/).

factor of a smartphone and is useful if you want stakeholders to discuss potential layout tradeoffs.

- **Cut up printed screenshots** into modules using scissors and ask people to arrange them in a single column on the table. This approach works well as a pair or group exercise.
- **Print out large screenshots** of the current website and ask stakeholders to attach numbered dots to each element on the screen. This approach avoids going down the rabbit-hole of discussing layout and keeps the focus on actual priority. (Just because we expect the logo or the primary nav to appear at the top of the page doesn't mean those elements are the most crucial for helping users complete their tasks.)
- **Display a spreadsheet** on the screen, where each worksheet represents one page, and each element appears on one row. Ask team members to rank the elements by assigning numbers. Ranking numerically by row means you can quickly reorder the list to get approval on the final prioritization. This approach works best when the team has comfortably completed a few examples using Post-its and is ready to move on to a faster process. (For distributed teams, you might share the spreadsheet in advance for people to complete on their own, then present an aggregated view of the rankings.)

Content choreography

Feeling good about your single-column forced prioritization? You haven't gotten to the hard part yet. One of the more challenging aspects of a responsive redesign is maintaining visual hierarchy and priority as objects flow across different screen sizes (**FIG 4.3**). (Right about now, you may wish you were reading a book called *Going M-dot*.)

Paravel founder Trent Walton coined the phrase "content choreography" to describe the process of stacking or grouping elements across different screen widths (http://bkaprt.com/gr/04-07/). Managing these "in-between states" lies at the heart of a responsive design process, and developers have a variety of technical solutions to achieve it—using media queries, flexbox, or other emerging layout syntax.

Stakeholders and content owners should not expect to specify exact priority for every device type or breakpoint, but getting input on the relationships between content elements can help with complex layout decisions. Consider including some additional exercises in your work session:

- Give teams the option to arrange Post-its in either a single stack column or two side by side. Which elements do they believe are at the same level of importance?
- Ask teams to draw a box around elements that should be kept together as a group. Why do they group those elements and not others?
- Tell team members they can draw an X through any items they believe should be dropped from the page at smaller sizes but kept at larger sizes. Why do they think these elements aren't always needed?

Benefits of content prioritization

These prioritization exercises can be time-consuming and painful—and ultimately worth every minute. The results of these conversations can inform and improve:

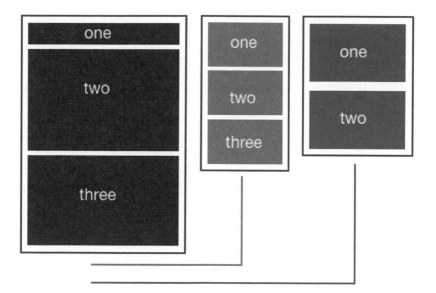

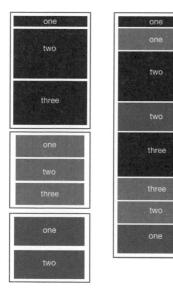

FIG 4.3: Three columns of a desktop website could simply stack on top of each other, but that doesn't preserve the intended prioritization of objects. Content choreography ensures that the visual hierarchy makes sense as items shift between different breakpoints (http://bkaprt.com/gr/04-08/).

- **editing,** by reducing or removing content deemed less valuable;
- **design and development,** by letting teams know which items should be more or less prominent;
- **site performance,** by ensuring that the most important elements load first.

When you prepared for your content prioritization exercise, you identified the content modules on the current site. That work will pay off when you develop a modular content structure for your responsive design. The process of breaking down content into smaller chunks is called *content modeling*.

CONTENT MODELING

I've seen lots of web projects focus on designing page templates. Designers plan layouts using lorem ipsum text and boxes with an *X* in them. The people responsible for the content get handed a variety of different layouts and are told to fill in the boxes. As a result, there's often a mismatch between the content and the design. That's why content strategists insist that content planning be included early in the process.

That doesn't mean that designers need to wait until every bit of content—every word, every picture—is gathered, written, edited, and approved. (If we worked that way, we'd never get anything done.) Rather, it means the team needs to have a shared understanding of the *structure* of the content before making decisions about templates and layouts.

Structure before layout

Content modeling is the process of identifying the types of content you publish, as well as sizes and attributes of the content, before designing your templates. This process frees content from its page-jail, giving it more flexibility and fluidity.

While content modeling and responsive design are two separate and independent processes, they fit together nicely. Organizations looking to implement adaptive content will need to define a content model so they can create, test, and display variations. (I go over this process in detail in *Content Strategy for Mobile*.)

The benefit of content modeling for a responsive redesign is understanding the size and shape of the content components that will sit within its flexible grid. Rather than starting with page types and layouts, teams begin by defining:

- **Content types.** What types of content do you publish: products, articles, recipes, explainers? What's the difference between an article and a blog post? I find that content creators are relieved to be given a chance to sit down and discuss what they create (and why) rather than jumping to how it will be presented on the website. Defining content types separate from page templates makes it more obvious that pieces of a particular content type can live on many different pages.
- **Content attributes.** I sometimes describe these as the "objects" that make up a content type: an article has a headline, a byline, a photo, and the article body. Defining the attributes of a content model separate from the data model in the CMS gives stakeholders a chance to weigh in on how they expect to create and reuse the content. It also gives designers and developers insight into the expected character count and data-type restrictions for each object.
- **Content relationships.** How will business rules and metadata be used to publish content dynamically? Too often, businesses copy and paste the same information on multiple pages, rather than storing content objects once in the CMS and publishing in multiple places. Defining dynamic content relationships is more efficient and less error-prone.

In the next chapter, I'll describe how companies develop frameworks or pattern libraries for their design systems. Consider content modeling as the corollary to that process for your content and CMS.

5 COLLABORATE

> " *Responsive is not a project. Responsive is a permanent new way of working.*"
> —SCOTT KELTON JONES, Expedia

I'VE SPENT THE PAST twenty years designing (and redesigning) websites. When I got started, a paper-first way of working made sense. Wireframes and Photoshop comps were the easiest way to communicate with teams and with clients—everybody had a printer, everybody could comment on a PDF. Here's how I once described my job: "You know what I think I'm going to do today? I'm going to draw some pictures of hypothetical future web pages and see if anyone likes them" (http://bkaprt. com/gr/05-01/).

But the old ways of working just don't work anymore. Pictures of web pages, constructed in Photoshop and distributed as PDFs—or worse, hard copies—seem like vestiges of another era, like watching a television broadcast of actors in a radio program speaking their lines. That's why advocates for agile methodologies or Lean UX recommend moving away from set-in-stone requirements, waterfall processes, and the fetishization of deliverables.

And yet, making changes so teams can work together in new ways requires more than an idealistic vision. Organizational structures often limit how people collaborate. New tools and libraries must be built or purchased, and they're not included in the budget or timeline. Stakeholders accustomed to working in a familiar process are resistant to change.

Responsive is your best opportunity to fix the way people work together. You may never get a better chance to change your team dynamics. In fact, responsive will force you to work in new ways—whether you want to or not. Frank Chimero, author of *The Shape of Design*, noted:

> *Everyone that I've spoken with that's worked on a large responsive project with a big client says that the process disrupts workflows, expectations, and work culture. Simply put, the edgelessness of the web tears down the constructed edges in the company. Everything is so interconnected that nobody has a clear domain of work any longer—the walls are gone, so we're left to learn how to collaborate in the spaces where things connect (http://bkaprt.com/gr/05-02/).*

Rather than leave your team to develop a new way of working on the fly, let's talk about how everyone's participation in the design and development process will change. Let me be clear: this section is not intended to provide a detailed guide for designers and developers about how their workflows will evolve—there are many other resources available to help answer that question, some of which appear in the back of the book. This section explains what everyone on your team needs to know to effectively collaborate in a responsive design process.

ORIENTATION

Plan to conduct an orientation session—or series of sessions—for everyone who might be involved in the redesign process. Think broadly about whom to invite, because QA testers, customer service representatives, and even lawyers will potentially be affected by this change.

While designers and developers probably have a good understanding of what going responsive means, you need to build a shared vision with the rest of the team. The goal of this orientation is to help everyone understand what will be different, what new language will be used, and what will be expected of them.

These are a few topics you might consider for your agenda. (You can download these talking points in PowerPoint and PDF formats: http://bkaprt.com/gr/05-03/).

- **Unfamiliar jargon.** What's a breakpoint? What's a media query? Teams may not need to know *how* to build websites using these concepts, but they do a need a level of comfort with new vocabulary. (A glossary with common terms appears in the back of the book and online: http://bkaprt. com/gr/05-04/).
- **Site traffic.** Do you have analytics data showing what percentage of your traffic comes from smartphones and tablets? That's often the most compelling argument for going responsive, because it shows just how important "mobile" is to your organization. You might supplement that data by sharing industry trends showing the rise of mobile devices and the proliferation of mobile platforms—even if your traffic isn't exploding with mobile visitors, your competitors' might be.
- **Mobile first.** Many organizations toss the buzzword "mobile first" around without having a shared understanding of what it means. Spend some time coaxing your team away from their fixation on the desktop and explain what a mobile-first decision-making process means to you.
- **Fluid designs.** Focusing on specific device types—mobile, tablet, and desktop—is meaningless when responsive designs are completely fluid. Yet stakeholders will fixate on these labels. Explain why avoiding device-specific discussions helps avoid making flawed assumptions.
- **Pixel perfection.** Stakeholders must move away from obsessing over pixel-perfect details. Not every device will get an identical experience, and that's okay. Your orientation ses-

sion should cover the basics of progressive enhancement and what it means to develop for all devices holistically.

- **Prototype reviews.** The way team members offer feedback on work-in-progress designs is likely to change. Explain how stakeholders will access prototypes from their mobile device or on shared devices in the lab (and explain that you won't be distributing PDFs).
- **Device support.** Even though you expect the website to work on most every device, you'll need to select a subset of devices and browsers for testing. Share a list of the ones you plan to support, and why.
- **Reporting and analytics.** While key metrics don't change with a responsive design, stakeholders accustomed to getting reports on a desktop website will need to look at the data in new ways. How will you evaluate the new site?

PROTOTYPING

Much ink has been spilled about the value of agile methods, iterative design, and functional prototyping. Some organizations have embraced these methods wholeheartedly. Others still cling to static comps.

Responsive can create a "lightbulb moment" for teams and stakeholders, because it's simply not feasible to demonstrate how designs will render and reflow at different breakpoints using static mockups. Teams accustomed to receiving documents or presentations will work together on reviewing functional prototypes. Joe Stewart, Partner at Work & Co, which teamed up with Dean Cookson, CIO of Virgin America on that company's responsive redesign, said:

> *Prototyping is our number one tool. Our philosophy on how to go about a responsive project is to race to a prototype as quickly as possible. We actually never once made a presentation, but we did constantly work on making prototypes. The very first time we got to meet Dean and the Virgin America team, we showed them a responsive prototype (http://bkaprt. com/gr/05-05/.*

A shift to responsive prototyping changes the way design and development teams collaborate and changes the way stakeholders respond to the work.

Breakpoints

Resize a browser window on a responsive website, and notice how the design reflows or flexes. Perhaps it shifts down from three columns to two, and then to a single column, or images and text that once sat side by side now stack vertically. These changes are defined using CSS and media queries, and the points at which the design shifts are called *breakpoints*. (The previous chapter discussed content choreography; breakpoints may be thought of as the way content choreography gets coded.)

In a responsive project, even teams that embrace the concept of device-agnostic design will find themselves pulled into discussing device types when the question of breakpoints arises. In an adaptive grid, the design "snaps" at specific sizes, but in a fully responsive design, the layout is completely fluid.

Breakpoints do not and should not neatly map to device sizes. If you've been following along at home, the reason should be obvious. There is no single definition for how wide a "smartphone" screen is; new devices come on the market all the time that defy expectations of a particular device type (hello, iPhone 6+!). Breakpoints are defined by the *content*—when line lengths get too long or whitespace becomes too big, designers decide to insert a breakpoint.

Your designers will also tell you that breakpoints don't all happen at once—while *major* breakpoints are defined to indicate major shifts in the layout, a number of *minor* breakpoints will also be defined to, say, manage small changes in the way navigation options appear in the header. A combination of major and minor breakpoints helps the responsive design work fluidly across all screen sizes, not just a handful of preselected resolutions.

Exactly where to place major and minor breakpoints is a decision best left to designers and developers—you don't need a team meeting to discuss them. But you *do* need a way to talk about the relationship between screen sizes and breakpoints. Here are some tips for doing that well:

- **Don't identify breakpoints based on screen resolutions.** It's tempting to look at your analytics data (or your iOS devices) and choose breakpoints based on known screen sizes. A content-driven approach to defining breakpoints places them wherever needed to make line lengths and image sizes appropriate for any screen width.
- **Don't talk about breakpoints using device types.** Trust me, you will have meetings where you discuss the "smartphone" or "tablet" size of the website. Trust me, it will be a hard habit to break. Trust me, you will be better off if you do. Device types carry with them a bundle of assumptions about capabilities and scenarios of use that aren't always true of a given screen width. Some teams get around this by using t-shirt sizes (or bears) as a way to refer to a broad category of screen size without implying anything about connection speed, input mechanism, or use cases.
- **Don't freak out about small differences.** When reviewing prototypes in context on different devices, stakeholders may agonize over minor differences in sizing, layout, or alignment. Remember: the goal isn't to have the site look exactly the same on every device. It's to create a website that *works* on every device. Don't waste time sweating the small stuff.

Prototyping tools

Many teams say they move into code much more quickly and make more of their decisions based on a working prototype. Dave Augustine from Airbnb said:

> This whole thing was prototyped in code, for the most part. We didn't receive Photoshop comps of what it looked like at different breakpoints. We received code, an actual functioning website (http://bkaprt.com/gr/01-45/).

Applications like Sketch (http://bkaprt.com/gr/05-06/), Macaw (http://bkaprt.com/gr/05-07/), InVision (http://bkaprt.com/gr/05-08/), and Edge Reflow from Adobe (http://bkaprt.com/gr/05-09/) offer prototyping capabilities so designers can quickly create responsive designs, review them in context, and solicit feedback from other members of the team, without requiring actual coding.

For functional prototyping and designing in the browser, front-end frameworks (a.k.a. CSS frameworks) offer configurable features—typography, forms, buttons, and reusable components, all within a responsive grid. Of the many frameworks out there, some popular ones are Bootstrap (http://bkaprt.com/gr/05-10/), Foundation (http://bkaprt.com/gr/05-11/), Gumby (http://bkaprt.com/gr/05-12/), and Skeleton (http://bkaprt.com/gr/05-13/). Teams often report that they start with a third-party framework and heavily customize it for their own needs. These frameworks can be quite useful for prototyping, even by people with modest development skills. (There are some downsides to using them for production code, but let's not go there.)

Deciding in the browser

Reports of the death of Photoshop are unevenly distributed. Despite the enthusiasm for prototyping solutions—what's been called "designing in the browser"—teams may find code-based prototyping to be slower than other methods. If you're changing your workflow and testing out new frameworks, you may need more time in the project plan for training and collaboration.

Responsive projects require new tools and skills, but your team can keep using the applications and workflows they're most comfortable (and fastest) with while testing out new ones. Teams that have adopted code-based prototyping methods still report using Photoshop, Illustrator, InDesign, and other static tools for developing the overall visual system and wireframes to present design decisions to stakeholders. Prototyping tools do not entirely replace existing applications—we need a variety of techniques to create great responsive designs.

Dan Mall famously quipped, "Let's change the phrase 'designing in the browser' to 'deciding in the browser'"(http://bkaprt. com/gr/05-14/). The point of prototyping isn't to have code-based methods replace the *design* process—it's more important that it modernize the *review* process. Let the team use whatever tools and methods it needs to get to a functioning prototype. But stakeholders should be expected to provide feedback on the prototype, gently guided away from expecting static comps for every breakpoint.

Scott Kelton Jones said he found that stakeholders from Expedia prefer reviewing prototypes—his teams never go back to static documents after they make the switch:

> *Whether it's me as I'm judging design solutions, or it's my boss, or it's the head of Expedia, once they see a prototype, once they see something being designed in code, people don't go back to static Photoshop comps. Once they get spoiled, people start saying, "What is this going to work like on the phone? What is it going to work like on the tablet? How is this really going to work?" You don't get to go back to static comps (http://bkaprt. com/gr/01-20/).*

Livia Labate from Marriott said that the value for them in using prototypes for reviews was faster turnaround and iteration. Teams would present work-in-progress, then quickly turn around changes—even updating the prototype during the meeting, which dramatically shortened time required for review and feedback. The functional prototype also meant that stakeholders could review and provide feedback at any time, without requiring a member of the design team to hold their hand:

> *If stakeholders have any questions about how users do X, Y, or Z, they look at the prototype. It's immensely powerful. People can access it at any time and they don't need me or another expert from our responsive program to explain how the site is going to work. They can just look at it, play with it, and they'll understand (http://bkaprt.com/gr/01-53/).*

Teams that use front-end frameworks and prototyping to speed up the design process and help stakeholders envision how the site will work often make the natural leap to developing prototypes and production code from a pattern library.

DESIGN SYSTEMS AND PATTERN LIBRARIES

Responsive design often goes hand in hand with developing a reusable set of design styles and components—sometimes called a *pattern library, design system, style guide,* or *framework.* The terms *module* and *component* are likewise used interchangeably (although component does have a more specific meaning in CMS development). Teams working on a pattern library should start by defining the language they'll use to describe patterns and modules (http://bkaprt.com/gr/05-15/).

While it's totally possible to implement a responsive design without a pattern library—and there are many good reasons for building a design system that go beyond responsive web design—having a modular framework makes the responsive design process go more smoothly.

Rather than starting with pages or page templates, teams first create reusable modules or components that are later assembled within a grid structure to create pages. These components are often described as "LEGO blocks" that can be combined in different ways.

Jeremy Keith from Clearleft, which partnered with Code for America on their responsive redesign, recalled that the pattern library was their main deliverable:

> *Some people call it a front-end style guide or a pattern library. Essentially it means breaking down the components of a page or a site into their atomic pieces and making sure that everything stands alone and works by itself. We deliver a collection of all those pieces as the main deliverable. We still provide pages, but pages are just examples of the patterns in action, almost like assembling LEGO blocks (http://bkaprt.com/gr/05-16/).*

If you remember the content modeling exercises from Chapter 4, this concept may sound familiar. The process of defining a more granular content model is closely related to the process for creating reusable design patterns.

I often describe three levels of modularization:

- **Front-end patterns.** A pattern library may exist solely as reusable pieces of front-end code, in a browsable format that explains how each pattern can be used. Rather than reinventing the wheel each time a new calendar widget or login form is needed, teams can grab a version that has already been designed and tested. But because the styles or code snippets are merely copied and pasted, there's no built-in management or enforcement of the design system—teams can modify the styles as they see fit, and changes to the system cannot be rolled out automatically.
- **Content modeling.** Design systems are often thought of as, well, design—a foundational visual language for common styles like tabs, buttons, tables, charts, and graphs. But as we saw in Chapter 4, content can also be structured and stored in a modular way. Like chocolate and peanut butter, design systems and content models go better together. If your pattern library only shows text, button labels, and form elements with dummy text, and your content model shows headings, teasers, and microcopy character counts, the next step in your journey is to fit these two systems together.
- **Backend components.** Components can also be implemented through the content management system, enabling designers and developers to construct and publish pages from reusable modules on the backend. A solid implementation means that changes can be made and tested on components, then rolled out across the entire system—much more efficient than updating each instance of front-end code. Capital One estimated that they publish 2,500 unique pages (encompassing a total of 4,000 adaptive page variations), but need only twenty backend components to maintain them (http://bkaprt.com/gr/01-39/).

Benefits of modularization

Code for America (http://bkaprt.com/gr/05-17/), MailChimp (http://bkaprt.com/gr/05-18/), and Starbucks (http://bkaprt.com/gr/05-19/) have all shared their pattern libraries to help other companies understand the value of these systems.

Focusing on modular pieces over pages has many benefits:

- **It's inherently responsive.** Flexible modules within a fluid grid system make it easy for designs to reflow across different screen sizes and breakpoints. Joe Stewart from Work & Co described the value of the modular system for Virgin America: "Anything that you do will automatically be responsive. If it fits in one of these modules, it will be responsive because the module system itself is naturally responsive" (http://bkaprt.com/gr/05-05/).
- **It improves consistency.** Page-based models can be wildly inefficient, virtually guaranteeing that sites will store duplicate content and display variations in design. Building and enforcing a modularized system means that content or design elements can be updated in one place and distributed site-wide, which makes it easier to maintain quality and consistency.
- **It supports prototyping.** Once the design system has been built, teams can quickly and easily create functional prototypes from the reusable modules. Tyler Fleck, Principal Web Designer at Expedia, said, "Once we published our documentation site that outlined all the core components, and showed what you could achieve by using the design and front-end framework, people really started to see the value of it in terms of how quickly we could assemble more finished UIs" (http://bkaprt.com/gr/05-20/).
- **It's faster to deploy.** It takes time to develop a design system, but once it's in place, a responsive design can be implemented more easily. Dave Augustine from Airbnb noted that their responsive relaunch was "one of the quickest and smoothest launches we've had" due to their front-end framework (http://bkaprt.com/gr/01-45/). Capital One pulled off a complete responsive redesign in just two months, giving all

the credit to their modular design system and component CMS—and their heroic UI Architect, Brian Dillon (http://bkaprt.com/gr/01-39/).

- **It streamlines testing and QA.** Components can be tested and validated once and then rolled out site-wide, which speeds up the testing and QA process. Brian Dillon of Capital One said, "The great thing about our site being so modular is that all we have to do is test an update on one or two pages and that meets the needs of our full regression testing. We don't have to review all 2,500 pages to know that the new module is going to work. It makes it a lot easier to quickly go through all those devices and only test what we need" (http://bkaprt.com/gr/05-21/).
- **It's cheaper in the long run.** Stakeholders get in the habit of expecting a custom design—their own special snowflake—for every single page. The BBC found bespoke page design to be much more costly than working with pre-designed and tested components. Niko Vijayaratnam, formerly Senior Product Manager at BBC Digital, stated, "It focuses people on the fact that creating new patterns costs time and money. Having a central pattern library, having that as the common language that we can all get behind, is really helping us" (http://bkaprt.com/gr/05-22/).

Design systems and responsive design

Teams that have wanted to create a modularized framework may find that a responsive redesign is the right time to do it—it's an easier sell when presented as part of a responsive program, as Livia Labate from Marriott found:

> Standards and a design system were things that we needed. But how do you make a business case to unify your visual identity? That's incredibly hard, especially as you compete against a hundred other initiatives and priorities. Unifying the visual system in the interest of making it easier to code and maintain our front end is a much more compelling business case. So things like that were absolutely possible in the context of making the site responsive (http://bkaprt.com/gr/01-53/).

Some companies find that implementing a design system *before* going responsive means the responsive design process goes more quickly. Rob Huddleston of Capital One said, "Let's think design system first. Design systems and patterns are probably the best place to start. They give you the most flexibility moving forward in terms of scalability and future-forward thinking" (http://bkaprt.com/gr/05-21/).

The challenge in implementing a pattern library is getting distributed teams to use it—rather than having them do their own thing or feel constrained by solutions that don't meet their needs. Marriott and Fidelity both have full-time employees responsible for their design systems. These team members lead monthly meetings to share new patterns and discuss changes to the system. They also oversee a governance process to ensure the pattern library is implemented as expected, and resolve issues that arise when teams need a style that isn't documented yet.

STAKEHOLDER REVIEWS

When I talk to clients about stakeholder reviews, they describe their typical approach to getting feedback from the wider organization:

- Teams ask for feedback on content in Word documents, which doesn't happen. Stakeholders demand to see polished Photoshop comps of every page.
- Photoshop comps get exported to PDF, then circulated via email or printed out so stakeholders can follow along when designs are projected on screen in meetings.
- Stakeholders provide feedback via email or in the PDF. Or by fax. Sometimes they handwrite comments and fax them. Everyone loves faxes.
- Feedback is provided on the design direction. And content. And functionality. Anything is fair game, really.
- Teams aggregate feedback and make changes. Ideally, this would be the end of the review process, but stakeholders demand a final round of comps before giving approval.

- Finally the work is ready to go into development. But changes to content from the last round of comps didn't get reflected in the latest Word documents. Someone's feedback (probably sent via fax) was mysteriously overlooked.
- Teams spend time tracking down and resolving conflicting feedback. Fixing version control problems seems to take more time than the actual design work.

When we talk through this process, everyone laughs, but it's an awkward laugh, like they're ashamed. During a break, meeting attendees pull me aside and hiss under their breath, "Our review process is broken. How do we fix it?"

Responsive design can be a forcing function that helps solve this problem, but only if you spend the time getting stakeholders on board. In the same way that going responsive requires a more collaborative, iterative process among design, development, and content teams, it also requires active collaboration with the rest of the organization.

Prototypes, not PDFs

Showing prototypes is the best advertisement for responsive design. Scott Childs of Capital One said, "We realized during the selling of this project that showing people how it worked and what it did, what responsive was in a browser or on a device, was what sold the project for us" (http://bkaprt.com/gr/01-39/).

Stakeholders may still want to focus on device types—"What does the tablet website look like?" or "My widget needs to be above the fold." The review and approval process needs to communicate that responsive design is completely flexible, and their "thing" doesn't "live" in a particular place. A prototype makes that clear.

Many teams report that they make a working prototype available on the server for comment at any time—which means that stakeholders must be made aware that work-in-progress prototypes will occasionally seem kind of janky. Stakeholders should be taught to look at the prototype on their personal phones or tablets—or on devices from the device lab—in addition to simply resizing the browser. Stakeholders may also benefit from using emulators, like the Responsive Web Design Testing Tool from Matt Kersley (http://bkaprt.com/gr/05-23/) or Breakpoint Tester from Macula Internet (http://bkaprt.com/gr/05-24/) that show how a site will appear at different breakpoints—though this should not replace looking at the site on actual devices.

Put new mechanisms in place to gather feedback on prototypes. How will teams capture notes from stakeholders and track which device, browser, and breakpoint the feedback references? Soliciting feedback on content choreography at different breakpoints will make gathering and evaluating feedback more complex. Prototyping apps like InVision are designed to simplify the feedback process by giving stakeholders an easy way to share comments. Jason Grigsby from Cloud Four said they use a tool called LICEcap to generate animated GIFs, which they use to solicit feedback from stakeholders (http://bkaprt.com/gr/05-25/). If you don't want to use a proprietary solution, you'll need to decide how you want to track and manage feedback at different breakpoints.

Devices, not projectors

During team collaboration and review sessions, seeing the site in context on a device is much more powerful than seeing it projected on a screen. Having a few different devices available in meetings is a great idea, especially if stakeholders don't have ongoing access to a prototype. Brian Greene from Nationwide described their device-specific review process:

> *Having the latest devices, the iPad mini with Retina display—so that they could really see what it would look like—got a lot of excitement with our business partners. Bringing in devices to show off the progress on the site was instrumental in getting their buy-in. Everything is so much more crisp and responds so well, it looks like the site was meant for that device. We did our best to not ever project. There were some scenarios where we had to project, but those projections are horrible, you can't see all the colors, and it doesn't really do it justice (http://bkaprt.com/gr/04-05/).*

Showing the site on devices is also a great way to encourage stakeholders to consider how the content will be presented, navigated, and read.

Legal review

Legal and compliance review either isn't a problem for you at all or it's your biggest problem. In heavily regulated industries like financial services and pharmaceuticals, going through legal and compliance reviews is always challenging, but never more so than when reviewing responsive designs. Rules for placement of footnotes, disclosures, and other bits of legalese are governed by requirements for print—which can be frustrating, if not comical, on smaller form factors. Legal and compliance processes traditionally require PDFs of desktop screens for review and comment; this won't be sufficient when the information shifts around in a responsive design.

Many design teams have worked hard to build collaborative relationships with friendly lawyers to streamline this process. See if you can find a "yes" lawyer who can help translate your design requirements to legalese and find creative solutions for this new environment—remember, lawyers use phones too. Legal and regulatory requirements will eventually change to take device types and screen sizes into account. Brian Hurley, SVP, Fidelity.com Platform Experience, reported that they're working with the regulatory agency to address this situation:

> We're literally helping the regulatory body rewrite their rules around disclosure, meaning how much needs to be shown and how disclosures are rendered in context versus in footnotes. This one regulatory body in particular has recognized that there's enough movement in the industry that they need to change their standards. Our legal team has been incredible in stepping up and helping lead that charge (http://bkaprt.com/gr/01-16/).

Responsive design changes the way people work. Teams benefit from a more collaborative process, which encourages different perspectives and puts the focus on building an actual functioning website. Many teams find this new collaborative approach saves time and makes the process go more smoothly.

So what are you going to do with the extra time you saved? I have some bad news: you're going to spend it all QA testing the website.

6 TEST AND MEASURE

" Every one of these responsive products we've rolled out have performed better than the previous products. We're actually very happy with it."
—**BILL SCOTT**, PayPal (http://bkaprt.com/gr/01-52/)

BY NOW, the benefits of a One Web philosophy for responsive design should be clear. Adopting design and development practices that embrace the fluid and flexible nature of the web allows us to avoid making device-specific decisions that add time, cost, and complexity when creating and maintaining the site.

Does that unified approach extend to research, testing, and analytics methods? If only it could be so simple.

In the broadest possible sense, responsive design does enable a holistic view of web success metrics. You want people to read, research, interact, and buy—on whichever device they choose. With responsive design, you can easily evaluate how often users achieve their goals across all devices. By not siloing development effort by device type, you also prevent unproductive competition for time and resources. Success for one platform doesn't come at the expense of another.

In a narrower sense, success must be evaluated—say it isn't so—at the device level. Even though the design and code is the same across devices, the user only sees one view. (Most people don't resize their browser window obsessively, I've discovered.) Device and platform-specific testing is needed to refine layouts and interactions—and find bugs. Looking at analytics by device type or platform will give you a nuanced picture of how customers engage with your site, and may help inform advertising and marketing initiatives, or plans for adaptive solutions.

So throw off that One Web banner you wrapped yourself in. (Admit it, it was getting kind of hair-shirty.) When we talk about research and testing methodologies, we must take specific device types into account. When it comes time to ask customers whether the responsive design meets their needs, we're going back to basics—back to devices.

TESTING AND SUPPORT

What devices and platforms do you *support?* In a simpler time, that question meant something: "This Page Best Viewed with Netscape Navigator 3.0." Adoption of web standards led to a world where websites worked pretty much everywhere—and a world where "QA" meant ensuring pixel-perfect layouts across all the various browsers and platforms.

Responsive means adopting a new definition of *support*, one that aims to make sure the widest possible audience can *use* the website, without expecting every user will see the exact same thing. This new definition of support changes how teams think about testing, because rather than looking for pixel-perfect layouts on every platform and screen size, they're focused on making sure users can complete their tasks—even if the presentation is different on different devices.

Jeremy Keith of Clearleft, describing their work for Code for America, emphasized that *support* does not mean *optimization*—they support everyone, but they don't optimize for any particular browser or platform:

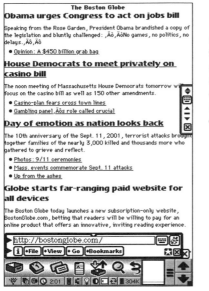

FIG. 6.1: No one at *The Boston Globe* tested on (or even considered) the ancient Apple Newton during their design and development process. And yet— overlooking a few character encoding problems—the site works (http://bkaprt. com/gr/06-01/).

We define support as: "Can you accomplish the task?" We think we've managed to give 100% support to any web browser capable of accessing the internet. That does not mean they all get the same experience—very, very far from it actually. Pulling it up in the device lab on quite a different range of devices—ancient Android phones, newer Windows phones, iOS devices—it looks quite different on all those devices. That's not a bug, that's a feature. It's good that it looks quite different on a four-year-old phone than it does on a one-year-old phone. It would be weird if it looked the same on both, that would actually be strange (http://bkaprt.com/gr/05-16/).

Well-implemented responsive design should function on all devices—even ones that weren't considered in the design and testing process. A new form factor like the iPhone 6+, a new device like the Android Wear watch, or even—surprisingly—a much older device like the Apple Newton should display a functioning responsive website, even if it looks different on each of those devices (**FIG 6.1**).

There are clear business benefits to thinking this way about device support. Rather than wasting time on ensuring pixel-perfect layouts across devices—an activity that never resulted in much tangible business value—teams focus on building a site that works on every device. Your future-friendly approach means you're already prepared when a new device comes along.

Support = testing

Just because teams don't optimize for a particular device type, screen size, browser, or platform during the design process doesn't mean the site isn't tested on actual devices. When we talk about supporting a particular device or browser, that means it's been identified as a priority for testing.

Monika Piotrowicz from Shopify said, "Support means it works across any screen size and any screen resolution. That's always something that we're going to be striving for in a responsive design." She went on to say that they're pragmatic in how they test in their device lab:

> *Practically speaking, there are a core set of desktop browsers that we support and actively test in. We have a mobile lab of some of the common mobile devices—and some of the less common but finicky mobile devices—that we can test on. We feel this is a good representation of the overall landscape, but you can't have every device under the sun (http://bkaprt.com/gr/01-17/).*

Building a device lab

Great, let's look at our designs in context to get a sense of how the site performs! Wait, where are we going to get all these devices?

If you're responsible for leading or overseeing a responsive redesign, you're responsible for ensuring your team has access to a lab of devices for research, design, and testing. Don't approach this ad hoc—have a plan for making sure your team can make good design decisions and evaluate performance.

- **Don't rely on online emulators** that claim to represent the experience on different devices (http://bkaprt.com/gr/06-02/). Emulators won't give you an accurate picture of how quickly your site renders, nor will they give testers a sense of what it feels like to interact with the device—though they can help for basic research and design purposes.
- **Don't rely on employees' personal devices** to compensate for building a device lab. Many companies assume team members will use their personal devices for testing, but don't expect everyone to bring multiple devices to the office. The success of your redesign shouldn't hinge on someone's personal device ownership—and the cost of providing devices is much less than the cost of ongoing testing, bug fixes, and customer support calls.

If you want to do this right, you need to invest in a proper device lab—so I'll walk you through the basics. For in-depth guidance on managing power, cables, user accounts and permissions, device activation, and lab security, you can find everything you've ever wanted to know (and more) in Destiny Montague and Lara Hogan's presentation on building a device lab at Etsy (http://bkaprt.com/gr/06-03/).

Selecting devices

Consider establishing a cross-functional team to select which devices to support. Marriott established a "Level of Support" working group with representatives from their research, analytics, content management, design, development, system administration, customer service, and QA teams. Each group might weigh in on the baseline and breadth of devices and platforms to be considered during the testing process. Because every device requires more time from the research and QA teams for testing and device-switching, the cost in increased time and effort should be considered when defining which devices will be supported.

Build your device lab gradually, and expect to purchase a good mix of devices. Smaller organizations may plan to acquire eight to ten devices to cover the basics, while larger organizations could collect twenty or thirty. Focus on the most common devices and device types, but make sure you're seeing the full range of platforms, OS versions, screen sizes, and input modes. Your analytics data should tell you—with an acceptable degree of accuracy—which devices are most popular. From there, make sure you're getting a good cross-section of:

- **Device types.** You'll want examples of smartphones and tablets, of course. Some teams may need to test on e-readers, televisions, or gaming systems—all of these may come with a built-in browser.
- **Operating systems.** You'll want examples of iOS, Android, Blackberry, Windows, and (Kindle) Fire OS. Depending on your audience, you may want examples of Firefox OS, Symbian, Bada, Ubuntu, webOS, and [insert your favorite open-source operating system here]. Don't forget about devices running desktop OS, like Microsoft Windows Surface or Chromebook. For Android in particular, and iOS to some extent, you'll need new and old versions of the OS running on high- and low-end devices.
- **Screen size and DPI.** You'll want a good range of screen sizes, from the smallest watch or smartphone up through large tablets and even TVs. You'll also benefit from having access to HD or Retina displays and standard resolutions.
- **Input modes.** While touch will be the primary input mechanism you'll need to test, be sure you have devices with hard and soft keyboards, as well as remote controls—even trackpads and mice. Don't forget to test on screen readers for the blind, too.
- **Browsers.** Remember you can install multiple browsers on each device for cross-browser testing.

Building a device lab may seem daunting and costly, but it doesn't have to be. Basing your device lab on older devices gives a more accurate picture of real-world speed and battery life—and it means you can build your device lab inexpensively. You can purchase used devices from eBay or other resellers. Some mobile phone retailers will let you purchase older devices at a discount. Team members may be willing to donate their old devices when they upgrade—consider offering them a gift card in exchange.

Making devices available

Making the device lab open and available to everyone means it will be used more often for reviews and collaboration. Rather than locking up devices in a cabinet, ensure that team members can easily check them out. (Use RFID tags to track device checkouts and assume there will be some loss and breakage.)

Testing across devices takes time, so give your team the tools they need to get the job done. Researchers and testers need priority access to the lab. Designers and developers should have at least two devices available to them throughout the process—most likely iOS and Android devices, in both smartphone and tablet form. While employees' personal devices are often the first line of defense for testing work-in-progress, encourage your team to check their work on older, less capable devices. And bring a variety of devices to meetings with stakeholders.

Usability testing

As with every web design project, you should plan to usability test your responsive designs throughout the process. Teams that have embraced an iterative process with regularly scheduled user studies will see the payoff in their responsive project. Teams that haven't adopted this way of working should consider moving to this model—not just for the responsive redesign, but because frequent user studies result in better designs.

If you're not already convinced that prototyping is the best and fastest way for teams to collaborate, another advantage of responsive prototyping is that you'll already have what you need to support usability tests. Participants can even bring up the prototype on their own devices, which makes the experience more personal and avoids some of the discomfort or inaccuracy with using lab computers.

When recruiting users for usability tests, you may wonder if you need to recruit three times as many people—say, eighteen rather than six users to cover smartphone, tablet, and desktop views. If you're conducting tests on a regular basis, this won't be as much of an issue—just prioritize the testing scenarios that require the most attention. If you're saving everything up for one or two big tests, plan to recruit a larger pool of users. If users look at multiple devices in a single session, randomize the order in which they see each one.

While the basic guidelines for research and testing stay the same, there are a few new tricks to consider when testing responsive sites:

- Content prioritization exercises can be conducted with users too. Like the stakeholder exercises in Chapter 4, you can ask users to rank information on the page or arrange content modules with Post-its. Keep it simple, since users will be less familiar with the content than business owners.
- Content choreography should be evaluated with potential users, especially when reviewing early-stage prototypes. Ask participants to review the site on smartphone, tablet, and desktop form factors; randomize the order in which they see each one.
- Don't be afraid to make changes to the prototype during the testing process—that's one of the perks of working iteratively.

A/B testing

Split testing or multivariate testing can greatly simplify—or complicate—the process of evaluating a responsive design.

A/B testing can make it faster and more accurate to evaluate changes. Rather than waiting for a round of usability testing, organizations like Expedia and Airbnb often run tests on the live site. Teams that have implemented a pattern library and componentized framework on the backend report that they were able to launch and test individual components gradually, without waiting for the site to fully launch.

Similarly, A/B tests may be used to evaluate and refine changes to the site content. Often, these tests are used to evaluate different marketing messages or promotional offers, but could also be used to test calls to action or even different content structures and navigation. If you're interested in testing

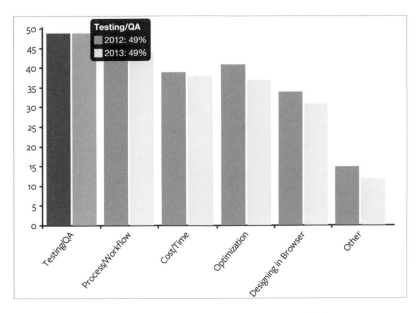

FIG 6.2: Testing and QA of responsive designs is the most painful of all the pain points, according to a survey conducted by Gridset in 2012 and 2013 (http://bkaprt.com/gr/06-05/).

mobile-specific landing pages or campaigns, you may wish to consider adaptive solutions over responsive templates (http://bkaprt.com/gr/06-04/).

Keep in mind that a performance cost comes with running A/B tests. While this delay may be relatively unnoticeable on fast desktop networks, users on mobile devices may suffer disproportionately, which can affect the results of the tests.

QA testing

Gridset conducted surveys in 2012 and 2013 to understand responsive design workflow (**FIG 6.2**). Both years, testing and QA was the number one reported challenge, with 49% of respondents saying it was their biggest pain point (http://bkaprt.com/gr/06-05/).

I won't sugarcoat it: QA testing of responsive designs will take longer and will likely cost more than testing fixed-width desktop sites. While design and development processes will speed up and stabilize—building responsive websites won't always take longer—companies should assume that the QA process will remain a pain point. Er, I mean, it will remain an *exciting challenge*. Running tests against different devices, orientations, and breakpoints simply takes more time.

Give your team and your process a break by not logging more bugs than necessary. Focus on what really matters:

- **Test scripts** should primarily evaluate whether it is possible for a user to complete a task. Required information should be available, text and images should be legible, and users should be able to progress through the transaction flow.
- **Visual QA** should ignore differences between platforms—layout, size, and styling will, by definition, be different. Testers will need a way to reference expected look-and-feel on various form factors, but the baseline for acceptability should be whether users can complete their task.
- **Prototypes** don't require the same level of support or scrutiny. Stakeholders may find that the prototype doesn't work as expected on lower-end Android devices (or Internet Explorer), and that's okay.

EVALUATION

While the ethos of responsive design embraces a fluid, flexible approach to designing across devices, most organizations will look at analytics and business metrics through the lens of device types, at least in the near term. Livia Labate from Marriott explained that they review analytics by device categories, even though their design process focuses on breakpoints:

> *We break down our analytics data across three main categories: smartphones, tablets, and everything else. That's just for reporting purposes. When we talk about design we don't use*

this language; instead we talk about breakpoints, because that level of granularity makes sense for the design process (http:// bkaprt.com/gr/01-53/).

Today, organizations want data that shows whether responsive designs are effective for different device types, whether there are problems or bugs at certain breakpoints, and whether they should invest in additional design or development for emerging or popular devices or form factors.

You know what else they want? Data that shows huge growth for key performance indicators on smartphones and tablets. If you've ever been in a meeting where an executive proclaimed an "eleventy bajillion percent increase in conversions on mobile!" you know that percentage increases on very small numbers can make reports look spectacular. Stakeholders will see political benefits from reporting large percentage increases on mobile.

Over the long term, it's likely that segmenting by platform will be less relevant to business goals. There will be no need to pit smartphones and tablets against the desktop (**FIG 6.3**). Rather than treating mobile as if it's a completely different animal, Forrester has found that the metrics used to evaluate success on mobile are the same as overall web metrics (http:// bkaprt.com/gr/06-06/).

Metrics

Typically, when embarking on a responsive redesign or evaluating its performance after launch, companies look at the following metrics—often by device type and by OS:

- **Visits.** The most common metric cited is the percentage of visits coming from mobile—often presented as smartphones plus tablets in aggregate. While this number varies by industry, it's not uncommon today for companies to see 50% of their traffic coming from mobile devices—and that number should go up after launching a responsive site. Companies with smaller percentages of visits from mobile—say, 10 to

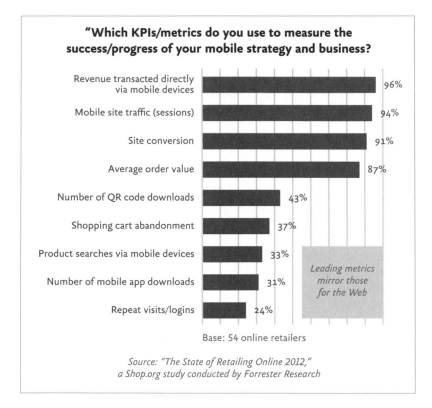

"Which KPIs/metrics do you use to measure the success/progress of your mobile strategy and business?

Metric	Value
Revenue transacted directly via mobile devices	96%
Mobile site traffic (sessions)	94%
Site conversion	91%
Average order value	87%
Number of QR code downloads	43%
Shopping cart abandonment	37%
Product searches via mobile devices	33%
Number of mobile app downloads	31%
Repeat visits/logins	24%

Leading metrics mirror those for the Web

Base: 54 online retailers

*Source: "The State of Retailing Online 2012,"
a Shop.org study conducted by Forrester Research*

FIG 6.3: Traffic, conversion rate, revenue—Forrester found that the metrics retailers use to evaluate success on mobile are the same as the web.

20%—are likely to see those numbers double when they launch a responsive site.

- **Bounce rate.** Bounce rate is another metric that gives a sense of user satisfaction and engagement on mobile. Users hitting a desktop-optimized page from a mobile device are more likely to leave the site immediately. Outside Magazine said their homepage bounce rate on smartphones was around 75% before their responsive redesign, but it dropped by 40% after they went responsive (http://bkaprt.com/gr/06-07/).

- **Time on site.** Engagement metrics like time on site should always go up, right? Not necessarily. While many sites will declare success when they see visitors spending more time reading articles or doing research, others may find that a responsive redesign helps users get in and get out quicker. Outside Magazine found that their time on site went *down* after a responsive redesign, because users weren't wasting time pinching and zooming. According to site director Todd Hodgson, "they're going to spend less time on your site because they're not battling your site, and that's a good thing" (http://bkaprt.com/gr/06-07/).
- **Page views.** Like time on site, page views may reflect users' genuine interest and engagement with the website—or a struggle to find the information they need. In the case of publishers, page views and their associated ad revenue are the primary goal. Scher Foord, Executive Director, Design at Condé Nast, said, "As we relaunch these responsive sites, we have seen tremendous upticks in uniques and page views for our mobile and tablet sites. We've seen two to three times the growth on mobile and tablet with a very consistent desktop metric" (http://bkaprt.com/gr/06-08/).
- **Repeat visits.** It's not enough to get users to visit the site once—in many cases, repeat visits are the real sign that people find the site useful. Capital One found that their repeat visits on mobile devices increased tenfold after their responsive redesign launched (http://bkaprt.com/gr/01-39/).
- **Referrals.** Many sites find that their traffic increasingly depends on social referrals (and to some extent email referrals) in addition to organic search. With Facebook, Twitter, Google Search, and email all tipping to a majority of mobile users—each of those platforms sees about 50% of traffic from mobile devices—a responsive website can help companies capitalize on valuable referral traffic. MTV responsively redesigned several of their properties with the intention of capturing more traffic from social channels. This work paid off in spades for the redesign of their show pages, which saw an increase of 246% in social referrals, and an eye-popping 565% increase in social referrals to MTV News (http://bkaprt.com/gr/06-09/).

- **Conversion rate.** Whether measured by actual sales or lead generation, this number should obviously go up. A report from Econsultancy stated, "I have yet to hear about a decline in conversion rates following the rollout of a responsive site" (http://bkaprt.com/gr/06-10/). Eoin Comerford, CEO of retailer Moosejaw, reported that their complete responsive design achieved a 50% conversion rate on mobile devices, matching what they see on desktop. He reminds other businesses: "You can't accept that mobile conversion is poorer than desktop conversion and that's just the way it is; you really do have to continually optimize for it" (http://bkaprt.com/gr/06-11/).
- **Revenue.** These other metrics are merely a proxy for what *really* matters to the CEO, which is increased revenue. Whether through direct sales or ad revenue, a responsive redesign should deliver real value. Skinny Ties, a family-owned and operated neckwear retailer, saw their overall conversion rate increase by 13.6% after a responsive redesign—almost 72% on iPhone, leading to 42.4% revenue growth across all devices, and 377.6% revenue growth on iPhone (http://bkaprt.com/gr/06-12/). Emily Smith, formerly Senior Vice President, Digital at the *Los Angeles Times,* explained that there were a "handful of new advertisers that we could never win on our old site, but that have—in some cases—made six-figure ad buys with us post-launch because we have such a better environment for their campaigns" after their responsive redesign (http://bkaprt.com/gr/06-13/).

Success stories

All this from a responsive redesign... Really? Well, maybe not. Successful responsive redesigns encompass so much more than fluid grids, flexible images, and media queries. By prioritizing information and features to meet user goals, streamlining design and functionality, and improving download speed, your site just works better. Mark Grannan, Application Development and Delivery Analyst for Forrester Research, cautioned that it's difficult to peg all these benefits directly to a responsive redesign:

So the question becomes: how do you attribute your increased traffic, conversions, or revenue to a single philosophy investment like RWD? The realistic answer: you don't. Instead, recognize that RWD is a facet of the overall shift to digital business operations and multichannel customer experience, while you focus on driving the most value for your customers and your organization (http://bkaprt.com/gr/01-25/, PDF, requires purchase).

Responsive design's benefits go beyond conversions and revenue growth. While those metrics are the most trackable—and are certainly key indicators of the health of the website and the business—there are other ways to evaluate success.

Nationwide reported that their salespeople are excited to talk to potential customers about their new responsive website and they're seeing an increase in sales as a result. Kevin Ackley, Specialist, Design and Usability at Nationwide, also said that the accolades they received from a powerful industry analyst made a huge impact on the company:

DALBAR is a market research firm in the financial industry. About three months after we went responsive, they came out with their quarterly review of financial websites. We went from—I don't think we were even ranked before that, to be honest with you—to number one in retirement plans with an Excellent rating. We're the only company with an Excellent rating right now (http://bkaprt.com/gr/04-05/).

A responsive redesign may also help reduce calls to customer support. By making transactions simpler to begin with—and enabling online customer service—expensive call center time can be reduced. Mike Donahue from Citrix said that they saw an immediate reduction in customer support costs:

Another way that we're trying to measure it is on the support side. Two of the key metrics we target are reducing call volume to the call centers and increasing the number of people entering tickets online. I'm happy to say the success of that has gone way beyond what we thought it would be. Phone call volume was reduced by 21%. Opening tickets online instead of phone calls has gone up nearly 50% in just the first thirty days. We weren't expecting that for probably three to six months, so we're really, really happy (http://bkaprt.com/gr/01-19/).

Perhaps the best benefit from a responsive redesign? Making sure that everyone gets access to the information they need, on whatever device they happen to use. 60% of visitors to AIDS. gov are on mobile devices. Miguel Gomez, Director of AIDS.gov from the Office of HIV/AIDS Policy, US Department of Health and Human Services, put it succinctly: "Responsive design is a tool to help the user." He continued:

> *Responsive design is one of the tools to help us constantly move forward, be faster, and get critical—not to sound dramatic— but get lifesaving information to people when they need it (http://bkaprt.com/gr/06-14/).*

Dozens of organizations report that a responsive redesign delivers value. Responsive solutions help create a more collaborative process, are easier and less costly to maintain over the long term, perform better in search, and lead to more satisfied customers and increased business value according to the metrics that matter most. Sounds like a worthwhile investment to me.

CONCLUSION

I'm a high-minded idealist about the web. I believe in supporting accessibility, web standards, and openness, because I believe these principles define this medium. The web isn't print or television—it's a medium unto itself, and availability to everyone is what makes it great.

I'm also a pragmatist about the web. I've seen enough teams struggle with limited resources and tight deadlines to know that my idealism only goes so far. I'm sympathetic to organizations that are overwhelmed by the constant pace of change in digital media, fed up with the endless demands of keeping up with new technology.

How lucky, then, to be able to advocate for responsive design—an approach that satisfies both my practical and idealistic sides.

To anyone who might argue that responsive design takes longer, I'm confident that this approach saves time and resources in the long run—reducing the burden on overworked teams and ensuring a process that delivers more value. For anyone who might argue that responsive design is more expensive, I need only quote Mike Monteiro, Design Director at Mule Design, who said, "It's going to cost you one thousand percent more *not* to do it" (http://bkaprt.com/gr/06-15/). Going responsive is a pragmatic solution for organizations who need to get the most from their limited time and budget (meaning everyone).

But I'm even more confident that responsive design is the right thing to do for the web. The approach presented in this book is an extension of the way the web has always worked. We don't need to fragment and silo the web to make it work across different devices and screen sizes—it naturally works that way, as long as we don't break it. Responsive design is simply the latest technique in a long tradition of making certain that the web is available and accessible to everyone, everywhere, on every device.

Whether you consider that to be an idealistic vision for this new medium or just good business sense, it's the right thing to do. Go forth, and go responsive.

GLOSSARY

Responsive web design introduces a new way of talking about web design and development. I present my personal—often biased—definitions for your reference. Don't toss these words around assuming that everyone knows what you mean. Discuss this glossary with your team to build a shared understanding of how responsive design is different.

adaptive — While responsive designs fluidly serve all devices with one set of client-side code, adaptive solutions require server-side negotiation to serve different content or HTML to the same URL, targeted based on device type or other known contextual variables. See **adaptive content, adaptive design**.

adaptive content — Structured content that can be targeted based on known characteristics of the user or the device. Serving different content to smartphones, tablets, and desktops is one common use, but adaptive content also supports contextual targeting (like location or time of day) and user-specific personalization.

adaptive design — Serving different HTML to solve device-specific layout problems. This can include device-specific pages (like a mobile landing page) or even device-specific functionality (like serving a different table to smartphone and desktop users).

adaptive grid — A series of fixed-width grid structures that snap into place at device-specific sizes, rather than being completely fluid, as in a fully responsive design. Unlike other adaptive solutions, adaptive grids do not require different HTML or server-side negotiation. See **fixed-width, fluid grid**.

breakpoint — The specified browser widths and heights where the layout shifts to rearrange, collapse, or hide elements on the page in a responsive design. Major breakpoints define significant changes in the design (like shifting the layout from a single column to two columns.) Minor breakpoints define small adjustments to improve readability or usability (like increasing the font size or adding more padding around elements.)

canonical URL — When the same web page may appear at multiple URLs, Google prefers that a single URL is selected as the preferred URL for indexing. To prevent Google from indexing the identical content on both a desktop site and an m-dot domain, a canonical URL defines which version should be used. See **m-dot**.

content choreography — Maintaining correct hierarchy of modules as layouts shift across multiple columns. Rather than simply stacking modules (so items in the right column at larger breakpoints wind up at the bottom of the page at smaller breakpoints), these modules can be interleaved at smaller breakpoints so they appear in the correct order.

design system — A defined set of grids, color palettes, type treatments, and graphic elements like lines, buttons, and image styles, which can be applied in different ways to create a more consistent visual identity. See **pattern library, front-end framework**.

designing in the browser — Using code-based prototyping tools in the design process instead of applications like Photoshop that provide static layouts. Front-end frameworks are often used to simplify this process.

device detection — Using a third-party library (often proprietary) to identify the device type and capabilities of the device. Device detection is required for adaptive and m-dot sites; responsive sites are built fluidly on the client side and do not require it. See **adaptive, m-dot, UA detection**.

fixed-width — A web page with a static, predefined pixel width that does not change in relation to the size of the browser window. Before responsive design, most websites had a fixed width of around 1000 pixels, which was designed to fill the screen of a 1024×768 monitor, the most common screen resolution at the time. See **adaptive grid, fluid grid**.

fluid grid — Responsive design is based on a fluid grid, where the maximum width of the web page, as well as the columns and containers within, are defined using proportional widths instead of fixed pixel-based dimensions. Objects change their widths and heights in relation to the size of the browser window. See **adaptive grid, fixed-width, relative units**.

the fold — Content placed at the top of the page that does not require scrolling to view is considered "above the fold." Because mobile devices have diverse, smaller screen sizes, it is less important to place information above the fold. Design techniques should encourage scrolling and ensure that calls to action are placed where users are prepared to act on them.

front-end framework — A mostly complete package of all the commonly used structures, layouts, and components that make up a website, implemented with standardized HTML, CSS, and JavaScript so developers can reuse predefined (but generic) code. See **design system, pattern library**.

graceful degradation — Delivers an ideal experience to users with modern browsers or devices, but offers fallbacks for situations where the ideal experience is not supported. See **progressive enhancement**.

hamburger menu — An icon showing three lines, which users tap to see the navigation options on devices with insufficient screen real estate to display the full navigation bar. Critics argue that hiding the menu under an unclear icon makes the site more difficult to navigate.

high-res images — Devices with higher pixel density (like Retina devices from Apple) require images with the same pixel density—otherwise the images appear pixellated or too small. Images with higher resolution are heavier and will slow down performance, so they should only be sent to devices that require them. See **responsive images**.

m-dot — Instead of a single responsively designed website, a separate website served only to mobile devices, usually served on a subdomain like m.domain.com. See **device detection**.

media queries — Enable the browser to test whether a device supports a particular media type and desired features, like a screen that has a minimum width of 780 pixels. In response, the browser loads different CSS which changes the way the content appears. Adding support for media queries to the CSS3 spec is what made responsive web design possible.

mobile first — Using the constraints and capabilities of mobile devices to focus and prioritize. By starting with the most constrained smartphone form factor, teams are forced to make choices. It's easier to start small and work up than to start with a desktop site and try to fit everything into a smaller view.

pattern library — A set of reusable interactive elements, like date pickers, pagination, or navigation styles, that developers can copy and paste into designs to save time and foster consistency across the site. Usually custom-designed for a specific website or brand and intended to be used as independent objects. See **design system**, **front-end framework**.

perceived performance — Techniques to optimize how fast the website appears to load so users can begin interacting. Sites that enable users to begin interacting more quickly feel faster, even if the page has not fully rendered.

pixel perfect — Coding and testing websites so they are identical across every browser. A responsive design does not need to look the same in all browsers.

progressive disclosure — A design technique that sequences the flow of information across screens, so users can focus on what's required to complete a task without being distracted or overwhelmed by unnecessary information. It is not the same as progressive enhancement.

progressive enhancement — Delivers a baseline of usable functionality to everyone, then layers on additional features or enhancements for browsers that can support them. By starting with the lowest common denominator and testing for support for enhancements before applying them, more capable browsers can deliver a better user experience while less capable browsers still deliver a functional experience. See **graceful degradation**.

prototype — Responsive designs require a prototype for making design decisions, rather than relying solely on static comps. Responsive prototypes often show only front-end behaviors, though some are integrated with data from the backend.

relative units — Responsive designs use proportional sizing, like percentages for widths or ems for font sizes, rather than using absolute units like pixels. Sizes of page elements like fonts or images are defined in relation to the size of the browser window.

responsive images — Because screens have different sizes and pixel densities, different images often need to be sent to different devices. New HTML markup attributes `srcset`, `sizes`, and `picture` enable developers to scale image sizes appropriately and provide multiple image source files.

user agent (UA) detection — Identifying the browser rendering engine using the user-agent string for the purpose of serving different HTML to different browsers. Notoriously inaccurate, as browsers identify themselves as other browsers to "spoof" UA detection. Responsive design does not require UA detection. See **device detection**.

viewport — The size of a webpage rendered in the browser window minus any browser chrome. Early mobile devices relied on two sizes of viewports: the visual viewport defined the visible screen real estate (say, 320 pixels), while the layout viewport was a larger virtual screen size (say, 980 pixels). This enabled existing desktop websites to be scaled and zoomed on smaller devices.

web standards — A philosophy of web design and development that encourages adhering to formal standards and practices for writing HTML, CSS, and JavaScript, to ensure accessibility and valid semantic encoding.

RESOURCES

Books on responsive design

Whether this book just whetted your appetite or you're looking for more in-depth guidance on designing and building a responsive site, these books will level-up your bookshelf.

- *Responsive Web Design,* Ethan Marcotte, http://bkaprt.com/gr/01-04/
- *Responsible Responsive Design,* Scott Jehl, http://bkaprt.com/gr/07-01/
- *Learning Responsive Web Design,* Clarissa Peterson, http://bkaprt.com/gr/07-02/
- *Implementing Responsive Design,* Tim Kadlec, http://bkaprt.com/gr/07-03/
- *Responsive Design Workflow,* Stephen Hay, http://bkaprt.com/gr/07-04/

Process and workflow

Every team will find their own ways of working, but it's helpful to hear how other teams have learned to work together.

- "The Modern Responsive Designer's Workflow," Dan Mall, http://bkaprt.com/gr/07-05/
- "Responsive Process," Ben Callahan, http://bkaprt.com/gr/07-05/
- "A New Responsive Design Process," Steve Fisher and Alaine Mackenzie, http://bkaprt.com/gr/07-06/

Content modeling

My favorite subject, covered by some of my favorite people.

- "Responsive Content Modeling," Steve Fisher, http://bkaprt.com/gr/07-07/

- "Content Choreography in RWD," Eileen Webb, http://bkaprt.com/gr/07-05/
- "The Core Model: Designing Inside Out for Better Results," Ida Aalen, http://bkaprt.com/gr/07-08/

Responsive images

New markup elements and attributes have emerged to solve the responsive images problem. This isn't just a technical solution—it changes content strategy and art direction, too.

- Responsive Images Community Group, http://bkaprt.com/gr/07-09/
- *Responsive Images 101,* Jason Grigsby, http://bkaprt.com/gr/07-10/
- *Responsive Images in Practice,* Eric Portis, http://bkaprt.com/gr/07-11/

Pattern libraries and style guides

This weighty topic could fill volumes. You will find no better resources to guide you through this complex landscape.

- Website Style Guide Resources, http://bkaprt.com/gr/07-12/
- *Front-end Style Guides,* Anna Debenham, http://bkaprt.com/gr/07-13/
- "Creating Style Guides," Susan Robertson, http://bkaprt.com/gr/07-14/

Testing

The art and science of testing responsive websites merits its own book—I hope someone writes it. Until then, take advantage of these helpful guides.

- "Prioritizing Devices: Testing And Responsive Web Design," Tom Maslen, http://bkaprt.com/gr/07-15/

- "Testing Mobile Responsive Design," Nicholas Potter, http://bkaprt.com/gr/07-16/
- "How to Test Mobile Responsive Design Applications," Matthew Heusser and Justin Rohrman, http://bkaprt.com/gr/07-17/

ACKNOWLEDGEMENTS

There's nothing like writing a book to make you appreciate the kindness and wisdom of your colleagues and friends. I'm genuinely lucky to know so many smart people and I'm genuinely grateful for all the help I received during this process.

To Jeffrey Zeldman, Jason Santa Maria, Nicole Fenton, Caren Litherland, Lisa Maria Martin, Rob Weychert, and the entire team at A Book Apart, thank you for agreeing to go through this whole goat rodeo with me a second time. Special thanks go to Katel LeDû for wrangling a miraculous number of goats at one time—and making it look so easy.

To Frank Chimero, I'm thrilled that you agreed to write the foreword. I'd like to add you to my professional network on LinkedIn.

To Jason Grigsby, thank you for ensuring I accurately communicated the nuances of the more complex aspects of responsive design. Anyone who needs help navigating a responsive project would be in good hands with Jason and the Cloud Four team.

To Livia Labate, thank you for generously giving so much of your time for interviews, advice, and reviewing a draft of the book. For my next book, I plan to follow you around and write down all the smart things you say; it will be a best seller.

To Stephen Turbek and Jeff Eaton, thank you both for reading early drafts of my first book, remaining friends with me, and then agreeing to do the same for a second book. You are true friends; there are none finer.

To Selina Andersson, thank you for your cheerful and unflappable help with this book—and nearly everything else in my life. Your assistance in scheduling podcast interviews and confirming quotes was valuable beyond measure. Thanks also to audio editor Aaron Schroeder and transcriber Seth Lavelle—two people I've never met, but who have suffered through endless hours listening to my recorded voice (and the sirens from the emergency room down the block.)

To Alex Breuer, Bill Scott, Brandon Rosage, Brian Dillon, Brian Greene, Brian Hurley, Chris Balt, Dave Augustine, Emily Smith, Eoin Comerford, Frank Punzo, Jason Chandler, Jeremy

Keith, Joe Stewart, Justin McDowell, Kalpita Kothary, Kevin Ackley, Mandy Brown, Miguel Gomez, Mike Donahue, Mike Monteiro, Monika Piotrowicz, Niko Vijayaratnam, Nishant Kothary, Patrick Cooper, Perry Hewitt, Robert Huddleston, Robert Petro, Ryan Shafer, Sarah Thompson, Scher Foord, Scott Childs, Scott Kelton Jones, Suzanne Connaughton, Tina Alexander, Todd Hodgson, Trei Brundrett, Tyler Fleck, and Zach Seward, thank you for sharing what you've learned from going responsive—your insights make the case more effectively than I ever could. Gratitude also goes out to every guest on the Responsive Web Design Podcast—your perspective helped shape this book, even if I didn't quote you directly.

To Aaron Parkening and Eileen Webb, thank you both for being so delightful to work with. I wanted to memorialize in a book just how great you are.

Remember sitcoms from the '80s and how the real star of the show's name appeared last in the credits? Thanks to Ethan Marcotte, for so many different reasons. Thank you for flying all over the world with me to help companies do better at responsive design. Thank you for not laughing at me when I suggested we host a podcast. Thank you for your insightful feedback on an absurdly early draft of this book and for not blocking me on Slack when I asked you yet another question about user agent detection on a Sunday morning. Thank you for inventing the damn thing. You've made my life—and the web—a much better place.

To my family, thanks for letting me be who I am without question. To all my friends (you know who you are), thanks for making me feel like I'm at home in every city I visit.

REFERENCES

Shortened URLs are numbered sequentially; the related long URLs are listed below for reference.

Introduction

00-01 http://responsivewebdesign.com/podcast/

Chapter 1

01-01 http://responsivewebdesign.com/podcast/seventh-generation.html

01-02 http://ben-evans.com/benedictevans/2015/6/19/presentation-mobile-is-eating-the-world

01-03 TK downloadable PDF URL

01-04 http://www.abookapart.com/products/responsive-web-design

01-05 http://www.marketingcharts.com/online/mobile-share-of-site-visits-by-industry-in-2014-52484/attachment/adobe-mobile-share-visits-by-industry-in-2014-mar2015/

01-06 http://www.slideshare.net/kleinerperkins/internet-trends-v1/

01-07 http://alistapart.com/article/vexing-viewports

01-08 https://developers.google.com/webmasters/mobile-sites/mobile-seo/configurations/dynamic-serving#correctly-detecting-user-agents

01-09 https://twitter.com/triblondon/status/558161890741092352

01-10 http://www.exacttarget.com/sites/exacttarget/files/deliverables/etmc-2014mobilebehaviorreport.pdf

01-11 https://www.thinkwithgoogle.com/research-studies/creating-moments-that-matter.html

01-12 http://services.google.com/fh/files/misc/multiscreenworld_final.pdf

01-13 http://www.pewinternet.org/2015/04/01/us-smartphone-use-in-2015/

01-14 http://responsivewebdesign.com/podcast/microsoft.html

01-15 http://responsivewebdesign.com/podcast/quartz.html

01-16 http://responsivewebdesign.com/podcast/fidelity.html

01-17 http://responsivewebdesign.com/podcast/shopify.html

01-18 http://www.retailmenot.com/corp/static/filer_public/78/9c/789c947a-fe7c-46ce-908a-790352326761/stateofmobileappsforretailers.pdf

01-19 http://responsivewebdesign.com/podcast/citrix.html

01-20 http://responsivewebdesign.com/podcast/expedia.html

01-21 http://responsivewebdesign.com/podcast/celebrity-cruises.html

01-22 http://responsivenews.co.uk/post/12647956085/traffic

01-23 http://www.w3.org/TR/mobile-bp/#OneWeb

01-24 http://futurefriendlyweb.com/

01-25 http://googlewebmastercentral.blogspot.com/2015/02/finding-more-mobile-friendly-search.html

01-26 http://www.marketingcharts.com/online/estimated-mobile-share-of-us-organic-search-traffic-by-engine-53937/

01-27 http://www.marketingcharts.com/online/estimated-mobile-share-of-us-organic-search-traffic-by-engine-53937/attachment/merklerkg-mobile-share-us-organic-search-traffic-q32013-q12015-apr2015/

01-28 https://developers.google.com/webmasters/mobile-sites/mobile-seo/configurations/responsive-design

01-29 https://developers.google.com/webmasters/mobile-sites/mobile-seo/overview/select-config

01-30 http://v1.aberdeen.com/launch/report/knowledge_brief/9084-KB-responsive-design.asp

01-31 http://www.flurry.com/bid/109749/Apps-Solidify-Leadership-Six-Years-into-the-Mobile-Revolution#.VQ3tFpPF-6A

01-32 http://linkback.morganstanley.com/web/sendlink/webapp/f/e49099bq-3pb2-g000-a9cf-005056028001?store=0&d=UwBSZXN
lYXJjaF9NUwBkMjYxMjIwMC02MDgwLTExZTUtOWNkYS0yYWVjNW
ZiMzM3MzU%3D&user=k8zaytx6tjb9-610&__gda__=1569211381_ddff0a
14f7abbe1454f722f9c78321fc

01-33 http://www.mobilemarketer.com/cms/news/research/19673.html

01-34 http://www.iab.net/media/file/IAB_Apps_and_Mobile_Web_Final.pdf

01-35 http://ben-evans.com/benedictevans/2015/5/14/apps-versus-the-web

01-36 http://bigqueri.es/t/m-dot-or-rwd-which-is-faster/296

01-37 http://www.exacttarget.com/sites/exacttarget/files/deliverables/etmc-2014mobilebehaviorreport.pdf

01-38 http://responsivewebdesign.com/podcast/capital-one.html

01-39 http://www.radware.com/mobile-sotu2014/

01-40 http://www.slideshare.net/guypod/performance-implications-of-mobile-design-perf-audience-edition

01-41 http://static.googleusercontent.com/media/www.google.com/en/us/intl/ALL_ALL/think/multiscreen/pdf/multi-screen-consumer-whitepaper_research-studies.pdf

01-42 http://searchengineland.com/the-definitive-guide-to-mobile-technical-seo-166066

01-43 http://responsivewebdesign.com/podcast/mtv.html

01-44 http://responsivewebdesign.com/podcast/airbnb.html

01-45 http://responsivewebdesign.com/podcast/npr.html

01-46 http://blog.froont.com/9-basic-principles-of-responsive-web-design/

01-47 http://www.huffingtonpost.com/garrett-goodman/
adaptive-design_b_2344569.html

01-48 http://www.lukew.com/ff/entry.asp?1392RESS

01-49 https://css-tricks.com/mixing-responsive-design-and-mobile-templates/

01-50 http://responsivewebdesign.com/podcast/beatport.html

01-51 http://responsivewebdesign.com/podcast/paypal.html

01-52 http://responsivewebdesign.com/podcast/marriott.html

Chapter 2

02-01 http://landing.adobe.com/dam/downloads/whitepapers/
53308.en.econsultancy-mobile-maturity-paper.pdf

02-02 http://responsivewebdesign.com/podcast/new-years.html

02-03 http://vimeo.com/88764543

02-04 https://www.forrester.com/Analyzing+The+Value+Of+
Responsive+Web+Design+Can+Be+Messy/fulltext/-/E-RES115961

02-05 http://www.elliotjaystocks.com/blog/responsive-web-design-the-war-
has-not-yet-been-won/

02-06 responsivewebdesign.com/podcast/ushahidi.html

02-07 https://en.wikipedia.org/wiki/Perpetual_beta

02-08 http://responsivewebdesign.com/podcast/guardian.html

02-09 http://responsivenews.co.uk/post/114413142693/weve-made-it

02-10 http://responsivewebdesign.com/podcast/vox.html

02-11 http://responsivenews.co.uk/post/79348308126/how-the-bbc-should-
practice-responsive-web-design

02-12 http://responsivewebdesign.com/podcast/chop.html

Chapter 3

03-01 http://timkadlec.com/2014/07/rwd-is-bad-for-performance-is-good-for-
performance/

03-02 http://www.sitepoint.com/average-page-weight-increases-15-2014/

03-03 http://www.webperformancetoday.com/2014/12/02/page-bloat-update-
average-top-1000-web-page-1795-kb-size/

03-04 http://www.uie.com/brainsparks/2015/02/02/jason-grigsby-real-world-
responsive-web-design/

03-05 http://httparchive.org/trends.php

03-06 http://www.uie.com/articles/download_time/

03-07 http://www.nngroup.com/articles/the-need-for-speed/

03-08 http://www.nngroup.com/articles/website-response-times/

03-09 https://econsultancy.com/blog/10936-site-speed-case-studies-tips-and-tools-for-improving-your-conversion-rate/

03-10 http://www.aberdeen.com/research/8491/ai-web-performance-management/content.aspx

03-11 http://radar.oreilly.com/2014/01/web-performance-is-user-experience.html

03-12 http://googlewebmastercentral.blogspot.com/2010/04/using-site-speed-in-web-search-ranking.html

03-13 http://googlewebmastercentral.blogspot.com/2013/06/changes-in-rankings-of-smartphone_11.html

03-14 http://www.webperformancetoday.com/2015/02/25/google-new-slow-label-web-performance/

03-15 http://www.smartinsights.com/mobile-marketing/mobile-marketing-analytics/mobile-marketing-statistics/

03-16 http://www.bmfms.com/documents/5%20Tips%20to%20Make%20Your%20Site%20Thrive%20on%20iOS%20&%20Android.pdf

03-17 http://www.webperformancetoday.com/2012/02/28/4-awesome-slides-showing-how-page-speed-correlates-to-business-metrics-at-walmart-com/

03-18 http://digiday.com/publishers/gq-com-cut-page-load-time-80-percent/

03-19 http://velocityconf.com/velocity2009/public/schedule/detail/8523

03-20 http://www.slideshare.net/cliffcrocker/velocity-ny-how-to-measure-revenue-in-milliseconds

03-21 http://blog.mozilla.org/metrics/2010/04/05/firefox-page-load-speed-%E2%80%93-part-ii/

03-22 http://velocityconf.com/velocity2009/public/schedule/detail/7709

03-23 http://kylerush.net/blog/meet-the-obama-campaigns-250-million-fundraising-platform/

03-24 http://www.guypo.com/responsive-web-design-is-bad-for-performance-there-i-said-it/

03-25 http://www.guypo.com/real-world-rwd-performance-take-2/

03-26 http://timkadlec.com/2012/10/blame-the-implementation-not-the-technique/

03-27 http://timkadlec.com/2014/11/performance-budget-metrics/

03-28 http://erikrunyon.com/2013/01/carousel-stats/

03-29 http://blog.typekit.com/2013/04/17/fallback-fonts-on-mobile-devices/

03-30 http://cognition.happycog.com/article/7-alternatives-to-popular-web-typefaces-for-better-performance

03-31 http://css-tricks.com/preventing-the-performance-hit-from-custom-fonts/

03-32 https://speakerdeck.com/ninjanails/death-to-icon-fonts

03-33 http://zurb.com/article/883/small-painful-buttons-why-social-media-bu

03-34 https://mobile.twitter.com/smashingmag/status/204955763368660992

03-35 http://responsivewebdesign.com/podcast/harvard.html

03-36 http://www.webperformancetoday.com/2011/07/14/fourth-party-calls-third-party-content/

03-37 http://www.webperformancetoday.com/2010/08/17/the-3-biggest-performance-problems-with-third-party-content/

03-38 http://www.webperformancetoday.com/2010/06/15/everything-you-wanted-to-know-about-web-performance/

03-39 http://www.slideshare.net/bbinto/third-party-footprint-evaluating-the-performance-of-external-scripts

03-40 http://clearleft.com/thinks/responsivedesignonabudget/

03-41 http://www.webpagetest.org/video/

03-42 https://blog.twitter.com/2012/improving-performance-on-twittercom

03-43 http://www.stevesouders.com/blog/2015/05/12/hero-image-custom-metrics/

03-44 https://www.forrester.com/Optimize+Your+Responsive+Website+Performance+To+Overcome+Mobile+Hurdles/fulltext/-/E-RES115962

Chapter 4

04-01 http://responsivewebdesign.com/podcast/evergreen.html

04-02 https://gathercontent.com/

04-03 https://draftin.com/

04-04 http://alistapart.com/article/content-templates-to-the-rescue

04-05 http://responsivewebdesign.com/podcast/nationwide.html

04-06 http://geovoices.geonetric.com/2012/07/content-considerations-for-responsive-websites/

04-07 http://trentwalton.com/2011/07/14/content-choreography/

04-08 http://www.smashingmagazine.com/2013/04/25/maintain-hierarchy-content-choreography/

Chapter 5

05-01 https://twitter.com/karenmcgrane/status/11754839838
05-02 http://frankchimero.com/talks/the-webs-grain/transcript/
05-03 TK downloadable PDF URL
05-04 TK downloadable PDF URL
05-05 http://responsivewebdesign.com/podcast/virgin-america.html
05-06 http://bohemiancoding.com/sketch/
05-07 http://macaw.co/
05-08 http://www.invisionapp.com/
05-09 https://creative.adobe.com/products/reflow
05-10 http://twitter.github.com/bootstrap/
05-11 http://foundation.zurb.com/
05-12 http://gumbyframework.com/
05-13 http://www.getskeleton.com/
05-14 https://the-pastry-box-project.net/dan-mall/2012-september-12
05-15 http://alistapart.com/article/language-of-modular-design
05-16 http://responsivewebdesign.com/podcast/code-for-america.html
05-17 http://codeforamerica.clearleft.com/
05-18 http://ux.mailchimp.com/patterns/
05-19 http://www.starbucks.com/static/reference/styleguide/
05-20 http://responsivewebdesign.com/podcast/expedia-two.html
05-21 http://responsivewebdesign.com/podcast/capital-one-part-two.html
05-22 http://responsivewebdesign.com/podcast/bbc.html
05-23 http://mattkersley.com/responsive/
05-24 http://breakpointtester.com/
05-25 http://www.cockos.com/licecap/

Chapter 6

06-01 https://www.flickr.com/photos/splorp/6141775264/
06-02 http://www.mobilexweb.com/emulators
06-03 http://larahogan.me/devicelab/
06-04 http://www.business2community.com/mobile-apps/a-mobile-responsive-landing-page-is-crushing-your-conversion-rate-01241051
06-05 http://2013.report.gridsetapp.com/
06-06 http://www.slideshare.net/KonySolutionsInc/forrester-kony-the-state-of-mobile-commerce-for-retailers-today
06-07 http://responsivewebdesign.com/podcast/outside-magazine.html

06-08 http://responsivewebdesign.com/podcast/conde-nast.html

06-09 http://www.lukew.com/ff/entry.asp?1939

06-10 https://econsultancy.com/blog/63185-14-brands-that-increased-conversion-rates-via-responsive-design/

06-11 http://responsivewebdesign.com/podcast/moosejaw.html

06-12 http://gravitydept.com/blog/skinny-ties-and-responsive-ecommerce

06-13 http://responsivewebdesign.com/podcast/la-times.html

06-14 https://www.forrester.com/Analyzing+The+Value+Of+Responsive+Web+Design+Can+Be+Messy/fulltext/-/E-RES115961

06-15 http://responsivewebdesign.com/podcast/aids-gov.html

06-16 http://responsivewebdesign.com/podcast/audubon.html

Resources

07-01 http://abookapart.com/products/responsible-responsive-design

07-02 http://shop.oreilly.com/product/0636920029199.do

07-03 http://www.implementingresponsivedesign.com/

07-04 http://www.responsivedesignworkflow.com/

07-05 https://shop.smashingmagazine.com/products/smashing-book-5-real-life-responsive-web-design

07-06 http://www.creativebloq.com/responsive-web-design/new-responsive-design-process-2132848

07-07 http://republicofquality.com/responsive-content-modeling/

07-08 http://alistapart.com/article/the-core-model-designing-inside-out-for-better-results

07-09 https://responsiveimages.org/

07-10 http://blog.cloudfour.com/responsive-images-101-definitions/

07-11 http://alistapart.com/article/responsive-images-in-practice

07-12 http://styleguides.io/

07-13 http://maban.co.uk/projects/front-end-style-guides/

07-14 http://alistapart.com/article/creating-style-guides

07-15 http://www.smashingmagazine.com/2014/07/testing-and-responsive-web-design/

07-16 http://www.siftdigital.com/who-we-are/testing-mobile-responsive-design

07-17 http://searchsoftwarequality.techtarget.com/tip/How-to-test-mobile-responsive-design-applications

INDEX

O

Obama for America 67
One Web 20
online emulators 115
OpenTable 26
organizational change 52
orientation sessions 95
Outside Magazine 123
overdownloading 69

P

page loading 61
page views 123
page weight 59, 77
pattern libraries 102
PayPal 39, 53
perceived performance 61
performance budgets 76
Perkins, Mark 76
Piotrowicz, Monika 16, 114
platform support 112
Podjarny, Guy 68
prioritization exercises 87, 118
prototyping 97, 101, 107, 117
prototyping tools 99
Punzo, Frank 56

Q

Quartz 16

R

responsive intranets 18
responsive retrofit 46
Responsive Web Design Testing Tool 108
RESS 34
rewriting content 82
Rosage, Brandon 44
Runyon, Erik 72

S

sandboxing 51
ScientiaMobile 29
Scott, Bill 39, 53, 111
search ranking 64
server calls 60, 77
Seward, Zach 16
Shafer, Ryan 32
Shopify 16, 114
shopping with smartphones 17
Shopzilla 66
Sillars, Doug 28
Skeleton 100
Sketch 100
Skinny Ties 124
Smashing Magazine 74
Smith, Emily 124
social media widgets 74
Souders, Steve 78
Sparkbox 73
SpeedCurve 78
stakeholder reviews 106
Staples 65
Starbucks 89, 104
Stewart, Joe 97, 104
Stocks, Elliott Jay 43
structured content 37

T

targeted content 38
test-and-learn culture 48
Thibeault, Jason 78
time to interact 61
training 55
Turbek, Stephen 16, 48
Typekit 43

U

usability testing 117
user agent detection 11
user research 86
Ushahidi 44

V

W

ABOUT A BOOK APART

We cover the emerging and essential topics in web design and development with style, clarity, and above all, brevity—because working designer-developers can't afford to waste time.

COLOPHON

The text is set in FF Yoga and its companion, FF Yoga Sans, both by Xavier Dupré. Headlines and cover are set in Titling Gothic by David Berlow.

 This book was printed in the United States using FSC certified Finch papers.